SCIENCE, SENSE & SOUL

SCIENCE, SENSE & SOUL

THE MYSTICAL-PHYSICAL NATURE
OF HUMAN EXISTENCE

Casey Blood, Ph.D.

RENAISSANCE BOOKS
Los Angeles

Quotations from the poet Rumi are taken from *The Essential Rumi,* translated by Coleman Barks (HarperSanFrancisco, 1994) and are used with the permission of the translator.

Library of Congress Control Number: Available upon request.
ISBN: 1-58063-219-X

10 9 8 7 6 5 4 3 2 1

Design by Susan Shankin

Published by Renaissance Books
Distributed by St. Martin's Press
Manufactured in the United States of America
First Edition

DEDICATION

I would like to thank Shahabuddin David Less for patiently, subtly, and not so subtly clarifying the essence of mysticism. And I would especially like to thank my wife Nurya for her invaluable encouragement, appreciation, and support.

CONTENTS

FOREWORD   XI

PREFACE   XIII

PART 1: INTRODUCTION

1. COSMOLOGIES   19

2. MYSTICISM   23

3. { } & THE GOALS OF EXISTENCE   29

4. THE DJINN PLANE   35

5. PHYSICS, NEUROSCIENCE & MYSTICAL PRACTICES   41

PART 2: PHYSICS

6. CLASSICAL PHYSICS — 51

7. QUANTUM MECHANICS — 57

8. MACROSCOPIC & MICROSCOPIC—SCHRÖDINGER'S CAT — 71

9. WAVES VERSUS PARTICLES—THE WAVE PICTURE — 75

10. QUANTUM MECHANICS & THE NONPHYSICAL MIND — 85

11. THE BRAIN & THE MIND — 95

12. PROPERTIES OF THE MIND—PURE INTELLIGENCE — 103

13. SUMMARY OF PHYSICS — 107

PART 3: THE BRAIN

14. INTRODUCTION TO THE BRAIN — 115

15. THE SYNAPSE — 119

16. THE COMPUTERLIKE ASPECTS OF THE BRAIN—VISION & MEMORY — 127

17. EMOTIONS—CONTROL OF ATTENTION — 137

PART 4: METAPHYSICS

18. THE ANGELIC PLANE—EMOTION — 153

19. THE JOURNEY OF THE SOUL — 161

20. DUALITY, LIFE, COVENANTS — 165

21. THE DJINN PLANE & MYSTICISM — 169

PART 5: PRACTICES

22. PRELIMINARIES TO THE PRACTICES — 185

23. THE WATCHING-YOUR-THOUGHTS PRACTICE — 193

24. BREATH, MUSIC & THE CHAKRAS — 203

25. PRACTICES PERFORMED DURING EVERYDAY LIFE   217

26. THE ART OF THE SELF   229

27. RETREATS, TEACHERS   247

28. THE PHYSICAL PLANE, BRAIN FUNCTIONS

     & MYSTICAL PRACTICES   253

29. THE MYSTIC & SOCIETY   261

APPENDICES

A. LOCALIZATION   273

B. AN EVALUATION OF QUANTUM MECHANICS   278

C. FURTHER THOUGHTS ON THE BRAIN & THE MIND   283

D. FURTHER DJINN THOUGHTS   288

ENDNOTES   299

BIBLIOGRAPHY   307

INDEX   310

FOREWORD

BY PIR VILAYAT INAYAT KHAN

When I was apprised of the honor that this wonderful scientist Casey Blood bestowed upon me, to write an introduction to his book, my first reaction was that I cannot imagine that a nonphysicist (or dabbler in physics) and an apprentice so-called "mystic" should confer any credibility to this work. Once I started reading his work, however, I realized the wisdom and the appropriateness for a scientist to ascribe credibility to the views of the mystics.

I am extremely grateful for the light that the views of scientists, which I assumed I understood, have thrown upon my efforts to understand what we are actually doing in meditation. Not only because it does involve physical processes (obviously connected with the mind), but also the updated paradigms of leading-edge scientists seem to corroborate the views that I pick up from the advanced thinkers of our times who are making contact with and adapting the views of great minds of all times.

•   •   •

Dr. Casey Blood fills a niche in the public's grasp of both physics and mysticism by presenting *both* in a readable fashion, so that their interconnectedness is made obvious without the trapping of sophisticated scientific theories and/or mystical paradoxes. I agree that even for sophisticated minds, however, it is difficult to see how a cat can be alive and dead at the same time. It is only a mystic who could believe that. So that in its simple approach, the Ariadne thread of the thinking in this book surreptitiously stretches the mind beyond in a single linear perspective. This is the very clue to "spirituality."

PIR VILAYAT INAYAT KHAN

Sarasota, Florida March 2001

PREFACE

Why did I write this book? The first reason came from my dual role as physicist and longtime student-practitioner of mysticism. What would happen, I wondered, if we assumed that quantum physics was the final theory of the physical universe, never to be superseded; and at the same time, we assumed that the best of the mystics have given an accurate description of the nature of existence? Could these two stances, the scientific and the mystical, be unified into a single consistent scheme, in which each complements and illuminates the other?

The answer, I believe, is yes.

In the course of pursuing this unification, I found that none of the many related books written over the last three decades, useful and provocative as they are, satisfactorily showed how physics and mysticism are tied together. The reason is that their views on the nature of matter are not definitive (Is it made up of particles? or of waves; or of . . . ?). Similarly, the mysticism they hope to unify physics with is not fully explained. Both of these, the nature of matter and the tenets of mysticism, as well as the connection between them, are more completely and systematically laid out here than they are elsewhere.

My second motive sprang from personal experience. For as long as I can remember, I have been interested in religion, but until I was forty, I only knew about the outer forms of religion and was not aware—at least not in a conventional sense—of mysticism, the root of religion. My hope is that this book will save a few readers from forty years of wandering in the desert of ignorance of the deeper forms of religion.

My third reason for writing the book came from my concern (and the concern of many others) about our society's personality-warping materialistic view that nothing exists save this obvious physical world. Part of the basis for the materialistic perspective is that science appears to support it; with its seemingly unassailable authority, science says that existence consists solely of material particles, and our intelligence and emotions are simply the result of the mechanisms of our physical brain. This view discourages many people from paying attention to their feeling that there is more to life than just physical existence.

Is science justified in putting this severe limitation on our perspective? It is not. Physics gives support to the idea of materialism through the almost universally held belief that our physical world is made up of material particles—electrons, protons, atoms—that objectively exist. After years of poring over the evidence, however, I have concluded that there is more reason to believe that particles *don't* exist than that they *do*. In addition, the biological sciences, powerful as they have become, are still almost infinitely far from showing there is no (nonphysical) director of the physical mechanisms of the body.

Thus science provides no support for materialism; it is not justified in limiting our belief to the materialistic perspective.

Finally, my hope for the book is that this attempt to dovetail physics with mysticism, to find the connections between brain functions and mystical practices, and to outline the bare bones of the vast field of mysticism will encourage those more mystically gifted and insightful than I to compile a modern spiritual manual—a map, along with travel advice, for the journey to the higher realms of existence.

PART I

INTRODUCTION

1

COSMOLOGIES

Where did I come from? What am I doing here? What is this strange feeling called love? Why are there wars? Are there worlds I do not see? What happens after I die? Do I have a soul? Is there really a God? We have all asked ourselves such questions. Almost always, we find no answers and we give up. Mystics—and in their own way, scientists—are the ones who have stayed with these simple, difficult, compelling questions. Their answers form the subject of this book.

The answers given here are embedded within a cosmology, a scheme or map that seeks to incorporate the significant aspects of all of existence—nonphysical as well as physical, mystical as well as scientific—into a unified whole. This cosmology is similar in many respects to the worldviews given in the major mystical systems and religions, but the interpretation of physics I use provides a more detailed picture of the connections between the physical and nonphysical worlds than we have had available before. And our current understanding of the workings of the brain also adds valuable knowledge. To incorporate this new scientific wisdom into a unified cosmology, we need to modify the traditional ones.

•   •   •

What should a cosmology explain? I suggest the following (with the mystic's views on physical and nonphysical existence kept in mind):

1. It should make clear the overall goal of existence—*why* that which exists was brought into being.
2. It should explain the nature and role of emotions.
3. It should explain the structure of the physical universe as well as why it is as it is.
4. It should give a perspective on the nonphysical aspects of existence and explain how they mesh with the physical aspect.
5. It should explain why there are so many apparently negative aspects of existence here—selfishness, coarseness, sloth, anger, violence, disease, pain—along with the positive aspects.
6. It should address death and birth.
7. It should offer insight into the nature of biological life.
8. It should give a perspective on the functioning and role of the human brain and why such an exquisite instrument has come into being.
9. Finally, it should give a perspective on humanity's role in existence, on the potential for human beings, and on how to attain that potential.

Almost all these issues are discussed in part 1, which is a book-within-a-book that outlines the cosmology. In part 2, I explain quantum mechanics, show how it implies there is a nonphysical world, deduce something of the nature of that world, and explain how the unseen world is relevant to our everyday lives.

Part 3 is a summary of how the brain works. This shows what is going on physically "behind the scenes" when we think and act our way through daily life; it lays the foundation for a more detailed understanding of how the physical and nonphysical mesh; and it is necessary for a full understanding of how mystical practices work. In part 4, I map out what the nonphysical world is like, so that we will have some idea of what happens when we die. (Quantum physics implies the existence of a nonphysical part to each of us. There is no reason why this "higher" nonphysical part should go out of existence when the "lower" physical part dies. It makes more sense to assume that the nonphysical persists even when the physical dies.) This knowledge is also essential for making sense of our lives here and is the first step in gaining experiential knowledge of the nonphysical world.

Finally, the aspiring mystic—the person who is not satisfied with physical existence alone—is also not satisfied with a conceptual cosmology (metaphysics); he or she wants experiential knowledge of the higher planes of the nonphysical world. To help you gain this experience, I have included in part 5 a core group of practices designed by both ancient and modern mystics. These practices are meant to draw you closer to the heart of earthly life, not distance you from it. They help you to attain your potential by changing the functioning of your nonphysical Mind so you can consciously experience the nonphysical planes while still alive. This is of great importance, for once you have experienced those planes, which are closer to the shattering beauty of the One, your viewpoint is changed—ecstatically changed—forever (*really* forever).

MYSTICISM

Most of us have a dual outlook on life. On one level, we simply do all the things we must do every day—work, eat, play . . . but on another level, we hope there is more to life—something that feels deeply real, a goal worthy of any effort, a grand overarching scheme. This hope is usually pushed into the background because it is so strongly discouraged by the materialistic values that prevail in our culture.

But suppose we do not wish to settle for a materialism that dulls our vitality. We might look for wisdom in conventional religion or therapy, or for self-knowledge in psychology and the workings of the brain, but these do not aim high enough. We might look to science with its hope of unraveling the secrets of the universe and providing for the material well-being of all, but these, too, are ultimately not satisfying. Where, then, are we to find what we long for? Nasrudin, the mythical Middle Eastern jokester-sage asks the same question:

> It's 4:00 A.M. Nasrudin leaves the tavern and walks the town aimlessly. A policeman stops him. "Why are you out wandering the streets in the middle of the night?"
>
> "Sir," replied Nasrudin, "if I knew the answer to that question, I would have been home hours ago!"

To find what we desire, we must dig deeper. We must discern the essence of spirituality; we must see what is beyond psychology and the workings of the brain; we must see what physics can tell us about the nature of existence.

And we must fly higher, until we have such an encompassing view that we can see the connections among spirit, brain, and physics, and ultimately discern the structure of all existence. When we can see this, and when we can begin to see why existence exists, then we will find a goal worthy of any effort.

PHYSICAL & NONPHYSICAL

The pivotal issue, at least in the beginning of our search, is the nature of existence, particularly human existence. In this scientific age, we are led to think that existence is strictly physical. If that is so, then it seems to me that life is indeed full of sound and fury, but signifies nothing. As we will see, however, science does not necessarily imply that existence is strictly physical. In fact, one of the basic themes of this book is that all existence, as well as each person, is divided into physical and nonphysical aspects. The division is sharp, but the two aspects are closely intertwined in our lives. Strange as it seems at first, we will find it is this division of existence that leads to a unified view of existence, a view that will allow us to make deep, satisfying sense of our lives.

These two aspects of existence have been explored by very different methods and disciplines. The experimental probing and mathematical description of the physical aspects of the world are, as we know, the province of physics, while the study and experience of the nonphysical aspects of existence are the provinces of mysticism. Mysticism in its various guises provides the core of all religions. The aspiring mystic is one who fervently hopes there is a nonphysical aspect to existence where worthy goals for our lives can be found. One purpose of this book is to nurture that hope by showing that science does not preclude mysticism, and by delineating the basics of mysticism in a clear and useful form.

QUANTUM MECHANICS AS THE BRIDGE TO MYSTICISM

If the nonphysical aspect of existence is to be of interest or use to us, then there must be some connection between our familiar physical world and the nonphysical world. The all-important bridge between the two is found in quantum mechanics, the theory that physicists use to mathematically describe the physical universe. (Rest assured that you will not need to understand anything about mathematics to read this book, nor do you need any prior knowledge of physics.) Physicists have a high degree of confidence in quantum mechanics because it gives a highly accurate, wide-ranging, and unified description of Nature, and because there are no known instances where it disagrees with experiment.

Quantum mechanics, however, has one astonishing "flaw." Although it is an accurate description of physical reality, its mathematics imply there are many versions of reality that exist simultaneously, rather than there being only the single reality that we actually see. For example, we will see in chapter 8 that the mathematics of quantum mechanics appear to allow Schrödinger's cat to be both dead and alive at the same time. To get around this "flaw," most physicists assume—without evidence—that quantum mechanics is an incomplete theory of the physical universe (with a complete theory being one that gives only a single version of reality), and that it needs to be amended to become complete. If, however, we do not make the unsupported "amendment" assumption, then *quantum mechanics implies beyond a shadow of a doubt that there must be a nonphysical aspect to existence!*[1]

Further, quantum mechanics tells us something about the nonphysical aspects of existence. It implies that each of us, in addition to having a physical brain and body, also has *a nonphysical Mind* (or *soul* in traditional language). Your nonphysical Mind, through its connection with your physical brain, can freely and intelligently choose your thoughts and actions. This is the bridge between the physical and nonphysical aspects of our existence.

The split within us that I stress—a physical brain-body and a nonphysical Mind—gives a dualistic existence. This may seem jarring in a book on mysticism, where the unity and connectedness of all things is usually stressed. It is true that in the end the duality disappears. The journey to the full experience of that unity is long, however, and on the journey, particularly in the beginning, the structure of existence is much clearer—both conceptually and experientially—if one stresses the dual nature of existence. This dual view is also consistent with that great duality none of us can escape—the difference between the physical existence we experience while alive and the nonphysical existence we hope or expect to experience after death.

WHAT FORM OF MYSTICISM?

There are many grades and types of mystics, from healers to whirling dervishes to the Dalai Lama to rishis living in caves in the Himalayas. And there are different systems of mysticism that have been developed over hundreds and even thousands of years in religions such as Hinduism, Buddhism, Sufism, certain branches of Christianity and Judaism, and so on (although most of these systems contain historical accretions as well as vital mysticism).

The system I will use is based on a modern form of Sufi mysticism that incorporates the wisdom of other systems modified to be consistent with the insights we will glean from physics and neuroscience. *Sufism* is an ancient way of knowing that does not correspond exactly to any of the better-known religions. It is a way of knowing that accurately sees and experiences existence from the point of view of the heart. Sufis are those who understand and experience all levels of existence, particularly those associated with the deepest emotions. A more traditional definition of Sufism would be that it is the mystical, esoteric branch of Islam, a branch that started with Muhammad's cousin and son-in-law Ali, flowered in the twelfth and thirteenth centuries, and continues today. An even shorter definition of *Sufism* is that it is the religion of experience. (A particularly perceptive statement of modern Sufi mysticism is given in Hazrat Inayat Khan's book, *The Soul Whence and Whither.* My metaphysics, except for the insights suggested by physics and neuroscience, closely follows Khan's book.)

It is my hope that making the mysticism consistent with science will clarify it so it is both accessible and appealing to many more people than it has been in the past. In fact, despite the materialistic bent of our society, I believe it is an advantage for the aspiring mystic to be living in the age of science, for as we will see, physics can help clarify the metaphysical structure of existence, and neuroscience can help both in distinguishing between physical brain-body effects and nonphysical insights, and in understanding mystical practices.

THE TONE OF THE WRITING

You may notice that there is a difference in the tone of the writing in the science sections when compared with the mysticism sections. In writing about the brain and even more in the part on physics, I speak as a scientist trying to *convince you logically* first, that science does not preclude mysticism and second, that quantum mechanics is compatible with mysticism.

Logical argumentation is not the tone of the sections on mysticism, however, because I am not trying to convince you logically that mysticism is correct (although I am trying to point out that mysticism gives a unifying perspective on existence). Rather I am simply *describing* what appears to me to be the most consistent and accurate view of physical and nonphysical existence. The source of this description, the "authority" for it, is the accumulated wisdom of the mystics (obviously interpreted by me).

If you are not familiar with the mystical point of view, it may appear simply as a belief system. But if you have the feeling it could be correct, if you think these ideas might serve as a useful guide for some period of your life, and if you do the mystical practices with your full attention on them, then I think you will begin to see that the mystic's view of existence may be experienced, rather than being just a belief system. You may begin to appreciate the possibility that awareness doesn't end with death, and you may begin to see that the potential exists for a radically different, much richer life here.

{ } & THE GOALS OF EXISTENCE

In the next few pages, I will give an overview of the structure of all existence—physical and nonphysical. Why is this relevant? Because that same structure is within each of us, and knowledge of it can radically change our lives. If we are not aware of the nonphysical aspects of existence, we can make no more sense of our lives than we could make of a game of chess in which we can see only four squares. And we can appreciate no more of the full beauty of existence than we could if we listened to a symphony but could hear in only a two-note range. If we don't know or understand the nature of existence, then we have no idea of our potential, and we lead lives that are only one-millionth as joyous and creative as they could be.

THE NAME { }

Before space and time and matter existed, there was "That," which was driven by a longing. That, that-which-brought-existence-into-being, is far beyond comprehension by our usual conceptual, brain-based, representational thinking and this complicates naming it. As the *Tao Te Ching* says:

> The Tao that can be told
> is not the eternal Tao.
> The name that can be named
> is not the eternal name.

But we need a way of writing "That." We could use a traditional name such as Yahweh, God, Allah, Atman, and so on, but that might prejudice our thinking about the qualities of That. To get around this problem, I will introduce a symbol, { }, for That.

The { can be thought of as representing Pure Emotion, expansion, receptivity, the richness of diversity, the archetypal feminine[1]. The } is Pure Intelligence,[2] contraction, activity, drawing in the essence of creation, the austerity of unity, the archetypal masculine. (We all, men and women, are a mixture of male and female archetypes. Male and female bring different attributes to existence, though, and it is useful to acknowledge that.)

The space in between represents existence, "that which is," including both physical and nonphysical existence. If you need a sound for { } while reading, you might use Hu, pronounced like the wind saying "whooo," and interpreted as "the presence left by one not in the room." (This is a sacred name and sound in both Middle Eastern and Native American traditions, and it is etymologically related to "human.")

PURE EMOTION & THE GOAL OF EXISTENCE

I will describe Pure Intelligence and Pure Emotion more fully as we go along, but briefly, Pure Emotion is the precursor of all emotions, all driving forces.

Pure Emotion is the cause of existence, and a full response to it is the goal of existence. The familiar emotion closest to Pure Emotion is longing for something akin to deep friendship or intimacy—a harmony and knowing and sharing between beings.

This cosmos-creating Pure Emotion has also been described by the prophet Muhammad, who said that "Allah is a hidden treasure that desires to be known." This implies that, in addition to friendship-intimacy, creativity in its broadest sense—*appreciated* creativity, because it desires to be known—is a large part of the reason for bringing existence into being. I don't mean just creativity in the arts, the sciences, politics, business, and other professions, but also in play, in conversation, in raising children. And it includes the creative diversity of Nature.

Pure Emotion, then—the driving force for bringing existence into being and the molder of the course of existence—is akin to both the longing for intimacy-friendship and the desire to create. The goals of existence—*satisfying the longing for friendship-intimacy and the desire to create*—are dictated by this driving force. (Obviously, these are the goals of existence only insofar as I can see from my limited perspective.)

For many ancient mystics, the only goal of life was union with { } (the highest, most rarified, and shattering form of friendship-intimacy), but modern mystics try to strike more of a balance between love of { } and love of { }'s creation—love of people, love of Nature. For them, *re*union after fully tasting existence is sweeter than unity. Modern mystics also feel that by developing the qualities of existence—majesty, power, beauty, wisdom, friendship—they can experience a higher union with { }.

PURE INTELLIGENCE

The other half of { }, Pure Intelligence, is the root of the means by which the goals of existence are to be sought. Pure Intelligence is much more vast than our usual idea of intelligence. It is what stands behind all our individual human intelligences, behind the intelligence of each being. And Pure Intelligence is the source of awareness.

How is Pure Intelligence related to our own intelligence? We usually think of the brain as the source of intelligence, but each of us also has an intelligent nonphysical Mind that directs, so to speak, the brain; that is, your own individual Mind freely chooses your own individual thoughts. It is the Mind that is the real source of intelligence; the brain is simply a tool. And that Mind is connected to Pure Intelligence; it is a facet or fragment or aspect of the single overarching Pure Intelligence.

This division of Pure Intelligence into many individual Minds is a way of carrying out "the desire to be known." Instead of having just one Being—Pure Intelligence—there are many beings and they can know and appreciate each other. Conversely, because each of us is, at our core, simply an aspect of Pure Intelligence, we are all interconnected. Mystics seek to become aware of that interconnection.

{ } & INDIVIDUAL BEINGS

"That which is" was brought into existence by { } as a means of dealing with or responding to the primary longing. Human (and other) beings, however, are not puppets that are manipulated by { }, *for the longing cannot be satisfied by manipulation.* (To see why, imagine that all conversations were scripted or that the moves in all chess games were prescribed. What would be the point?) Instead, each being has autonomy, responsibility (within a certain sphere) for its own actions. There is indeed an overarching scheme for existence, but, because existence is not puppetlike or rigidly specified, there is no hard and fast plan. Instead, existence is being *actively created* at each instant of time.

Who creates? In this nonpuppetlike cosmology, { } participates only indirectly.

{ } has laid down certain principles or secondary goals (after friendship-intimacy and creativity) that human beings may follow, if they choose, in order to satisfy the longing. Some of these take the form of attributes or qualities which, if developed, lead to an existence that satisfies the longing. That is, to achieve the goals that { } has in mind for existence, each of us could become a being of great magnificence, beauty, power, wisdom, insight, creativity, a being who embodies love and friendship. So, here on earth, { } seeks to fulfill the goals of existence through our freely chosen human actions. (I must add, however, that the full story is more complex. There are beings, intermediaries between humans and { }, who can, to some extent, "guide" human affairs, so that we are not always the *only* creators.)

We might ask how we are related to { }. In Islam and Sufism, it is said that "Nothing exists save Allah" (or in our terms, "nothing exists save { }"). That is, there is nothing—including each of us—that is not, in some sense, { }. We are, however, an aspect of { } that is not aware of all existence; we are aware only of a very small corner of our physical world. And so we cannot claim in any meaningful sense to be { }. (Nor, for that matter, can we claim to be not { }.)

"IMPERFECTION"

Because existence is not puppetlike, there is no assurance that what we do will help move us toward the goals of friendship-intimacy and creativity. We may be so fixated on our own desires that we offend others rather than befriending them. Or we may have such a need for stability that we live life in a habitual, noncreative, way. Moving toward friendship-intimacy and creativity is not automatic; it requires work, some minimal set of fortuitous circumstances, and vision that looks beyond small, temporary satisfactions. Because these conditions are not always met, there are times in our lives when we do not discernibly move toward the goals that { } hopes for. By the same reasoning, but on a larger scale, there are also societal situations—war, poverty, disease—where we seem to make no progress. So the miseries of this world occur, not because { } is bad or indifferent, but because the rules of the game of existence—that is, the freedom { } had to give to individuals to make existence worthwhile—require that power be given to beings who are not fully wise and unselfish.

Thus, from the suppositions of this cosmology—that there are no guarantees of success and that there are negative aspects to existence—we see that { } is different from the central figures of some religions. { } is not an all-powerful God who makes happen whatever she or he chooses. Nor is { } perfect—perfect in justice, compassion, and wisdom. Why? Because { } finds it necessary, in attempting to satisfy the longing, to function through us, with all our inevitable weaknesses and lack of vision.

To prevent this idea of the "imperfection" of { } from giving the wrong impression, however, we must remember that { } is all-powerful in the sense that all existence springs from Her or Him. One might also say that perfect and imperfect are irrelevant when describing { }, however, for there is nothing against which to judge perfection when referring to the one who brings existence into being; our human standards of judgment are simply not relevant here. Also, perfection is not really the issue when true longing or loving is involved.

THE DJINN PLANE

What happens after we die? Most of us have a vague hope that we will continue to exist in some form. But the mystic can tell us more, much more, for
after we die we are in the nonphysical realms, and that is the mystic's domain.

Our world here, the physical world we are familiar with, is called the physical plane. The place we go after we die is called the *djinn* (silent *d,* rhymes with
spin, etymologically related to *genie, genius*) plane in this cosmology. Dreams
give us some idea of how existence there will feel. There is no concrete reality
as there is here; faces, places, even the story line can change in an instant.
Emotion assumes a more prominent role than logic, and, if we are not mystically prepared or innocent as a child when we die, we have relatively little
control over events.

A description of existence on that plane is given in *The Tibetan Book of Living and Dying* by Sogyal Rinpoche. In this description, the bardo of becoming is the Tibetan phrase for the part of the djinn plane where beings who have died reside, and the mental body is the form one has there. This applies to an average person—one not mystically developed—who has recently died:

> Our mental body in the bardo of becoming has a number of special characteristics. It possesses all its senses. It is extremely light, lucid and mobile, and its awareness is said to be seven times clearer than in life. It is also endowed with a rudimentary kind of clairvoyance, which is not under conscious control, but gives the mental body the ability to read others' minds . . . The mental body is unable to remain still, even for an instant. It is ceaselessly on the move . . . In this state, mental activity is very rapid: thoughts come in quick succession, and we can do many things at once. *The mind continues to perpetuate set patterns and habits . . .* [emphasis added].

DJINN THOUGHTS—LIFE AFTER DEATH

Each plane is defined by the types of "material" or "forms" that make up existence on that plane. On the physical plane, the forms are our familiar physical forms—bodies, rocks, trees, clouds, stars, and so on. On the djinn plane, the forms are similar to, but not the same as, our dreams and thoughts, so we call them djinn thoughts, or djinn thought-forms. (These are in the same ballpark as Plato's ideal forms that exist in the world of being—as opposed to the experiential world of becoming. His knowledge of them came from his mystical insight.) The djinn plane is constructed from djinn thought-forms, just as the physical world is made up of physical forms.

There are many different kinds of djinn thought-forms. Some of them form the background for our world here, although we are seldom (or more likely, never) conscious of them. There are djinn thought-forms corresponding to all the objects of our physical world—dogs, deserts, desktops. There are djinn thought-forms corresponding to music, mathematics, art, poetry, sex, and all the concepts of our world, although they are not as concrete and unambiguous as concepts are here. Thus there is a part of the djinn plane—that is, a category of djinn thought-forms—that is closely related to life on earth. It is these earth-related djinn thought-forms that we will experience on the djinn plane for some time after our death.

As indicated in the quote from *The Tibetan Book of Living and Dying*—"The mind continues to perpetuate set patterns and habits," the nature of our after-death experience on the djinn plane will depend on how we conduct our lives here. If we dwell on anger, fear, jealousy, and greed here, we will, in a kind of hell, dwell on these same thought-emotions there. But it will be much worse there because there is no concrete physical reality to break the emotions and "bring us back down to earth." (Rumi delicately says it's circumcision here but full castration there.) Conversely, if our thoughts here are loving and harmonious, the djinn plane will become heaven. This may sound like old-fashioned hellfire and brimstone preaching, but it's just the way existence is; our mindset here stays with us there and is even magnified.

The djinn plane contains much more than just the djinn thought-forms related to our physical life here. There are other realms, realms that have no analog here but that we can sense when watching a sunset, listening to sublime music, or making love. After death, we will gradually become aware of those other realms (which are made up of djinn thought-forms that are very different from those that form the background of our physical world).

BEINGS ON THE DJINN PLANE—LIFE BEFORE BIRTH

There are beings that dwell on the djinn plane and are aware of the djinn thought-forms there, just as we are aware of our physical world here; each of us will become one of those beings when we die. We will be able to find and communicate with our friends who have died.

In addition to those who have died, there are other beings who inhabit the djinn plane (that is, beings who are aware of djinn thought-forms). *Each of us lived there before we were born,* so we already have a history at the moment of conception.

There is, however, no reincarnation in this cosmology; we do not move back and forth many times between the djinn and physical planes. Why then are some people born with specific inclinations, interests, and mindsets? Because those who have died and reentered the djinn plane communicate with those not yet born. So, for example, someone about to be born might "speak" with Beethoven's djinn being and pick up something of his musical inclination. (There may be special circumstances in this cosmology—having excellent mystical knowledge and a very strong desire to serve humanity, for example—under which reincarnation is possible.)

THE DJINN PLANE & LIFE ON EARTH

Is the djinn plane relevant for life on earth? Yes, it is. First, it provides an underpinning or template for both physical objects and concepts. Second, it provides the mechanisms for what we think of as supernormal (or paranormal) phenomena: healing, knowledge of the virtues of plants, mind reading, perceiving the past, foreseeing the future, manipulating events—yes, these really do occur—all take place through the djinn plane. Mystics automatically acquire a basic form of many of these skills as they progress, and they can become more proficient in a given skill if they deem it important.

Further, there are influences from the djinn plane that can affect us here. For example, they can obscure an obvious truth for a time or they can make us more or less inclined toward peace (but I am not suggesting that we have no responsibility for our actions). Mystics can perceive these influences and make sure their judgment is not clouded by them.

Why can mystics perceive and act on the djinn plane? Are they special? They are not special because conscious perception on the djinn plane is possible for us all; each of us, in addition to our physical body, also has a djinn "body" that can perceive djinn thought-forms. The thing that makes the mystics different is that they have done practices that allow them to perceive on the djinn plane and become consciously aware of djinn thought-forms. And mystics are different because they experience a wonder and joy in being able to consciously experience the djinn plane, which is closer to { } than our physical plane.

•   •   •

I will speak of the djinn plane as being "above" the physical plane because, in addition to its being closer to { }, everything that exists on the physical plane depends on a djinn thought-form for its existence. There is also one other plane, above the djinn plane, called the *angelic* plane, but it is more abstract than the djinn plane so I will postpone its description until later.

PHYSICS, NEUROSCIENCE & MYSTICAL PRACTICES

This book sets out to accomplish two things: to *describe* the nature of human existence on the physical and nonphysical planes and to give practices that help those who do them to *experience* all the levels of existence. In the last chapter, I indicated that we currently exist on both the physical and djinn planes, and I gave a basic description of the djinn plane. In the following I will describe the nature of our existence here on the physical plane in a way that is relevant for mysticism, and then say a few words about the practices that lead toward mystical experience.

TWO PERSPECTIVES ON PHYSICS

Over the past four hundred years, physicists have probed the world through millions of experiments. The results of these experiments have been summarized in the mathematical laws and theories of physics. These theories have become so unified that there are now only two equations (at the atomic level) that correctly describe, as far as we know, all of physical existence. These two equations are the heart of quantum mechanics, the theory that is universally accepted as giving a correct mathematical description of Nature. In fact, because quantum mechanics describes the physical universe so well, we *define* the physical universe as that which obeys the equations of quantum mechanics.

As I said earlier, however, quantum mechanics has a most interesting peculiarity. Its mathematics allows many versions of reality instead of the single one we perceive. How do physicists cope with the seeming paradox that a theory that is undoubtedly correct in every other respect gives more than one reality? Their point of view is normally the following: The mathematics of quantum mechanics does indeed allow many versions of reality, but we perceive only one. Therefore, even though it is correct, quantum mechanics must not be a complete theory of the physical universe, for because we *see* only one version of reality, then in the complete mathematical description of Nature, there must *be* only one version of reality. That is, quantum mechanics needs to be amended to be a complete theory.

This is the stance of the physicist. What about the mystic? The mystic says the physicist's "amended" view of quantum mechanics leaves no room for a nonphysical component to existence and so there must be a different way of understanding the physics. And indeed there is. The key is that there is no evidence that the physicist's idea—that quantum mechanics needs to be amended—is correct. So we are free to assume, in the absence of evidence to the contrary, that quantum mechanics is a complete description of the physical universe and that all the many futures "actually occur." How is this to be reconciled with the fact that we know from experience that we see only one of the versions of reality? It is reconciled by supposing that we *perceive* only one version, even though many occur.

Incomplete or not, quantum mechanics has no known failures, and it must be reckoned with. We have our choice of how to reckon with it: We can say, with no evidence, that it is incomplete: or we can take the mathematics at face value and say that it is complete. We take it at face value, so that all the versions of reality exist but we see only one.

This is most important for mysticism, for it implies—as I will show later— that *that which sees only one version of reality must be outside the physical universe, nonphysical.* This result gives us the connection between the physical and the nonphysical aspects of existence.[1]

TWO PERSPECTIVES ON THE MIND

Modern neuroscience is only one hundred fifty or so years old, much younger than physics, because it is difficult to study the brain. But we have learned a great deal in that time. Neuroscientists know that the many mental processes we employ are localized at different places in the brain. For example, those regions that make sense of sight are located on the back surface of the brain, those we use for touch are located on the surface of the brain near the middle of the head, the regions associated with emotions are located in the center of the brain, and those regions where we think and make sense of it all are located on the front surface of the brain. And neuroscientists know that the neurochemicals that affect thinking and moods—nicotine, caffeine, alcohol, and so on—work at the junctions between the nerves that make up the brain.

This knowledge has led to a certain point of view on the brain in particular and human beings in general. Many neuroscientists believe their knowledge of the workings of the brain shows that it is nothing but a sophisticated computer; there is no operator of the computer, no soul behind the computer, just the computer. This point of view, along with the physicists' view of physical reality, is called materialism—the belief that *nothing exists but the material world our senses perceive.*

Because the mystic can actually perceive the nonphysical world and see how it affects the world here, however, he or she knows that this view is incorrect. The mystic says that neuroscientists have drawn a conclusion their knowledge does not support. The brain has indeed been found to be an amazing machine, but there is no data whatsoever that precludes there being an operator of the machine, a Mind behind the machine.

Most Westerners today embrace a materialistic view of the world—there is no soul, no life after death; there is only this material world evident to our physical senses. (And the inference often drawn is that we had best concentrate our efforts on obtaining as many material goods and pleasurable experiences as we can.) Science is often used to justify this view, but it cannot; there is no convincing evidence from neuroscience that there is no nonphysical "director" of our brain activities. Moreover, as we will see, there is no convincing evidence from physics that particles—the presumed building blocks of the material world—exist. Thus there is no credible support for the philosophy that underlies much of modern Western culture at this time.

THE PERSPECTIVE OF { } ON PHYSICAL EXISTENCE

I have given a view of existence from the perspective of the physicist, the neuroscientist, and the mystic. There is one more perspective on our physical existence that we should be familiar with, that of { }.

To help attain the goals of existence, { } thought it necessary to create a part of existence—the physical plane—where there was order and concreteness and, at the same time, freedom. { } decided to impose order on this existence by basing it on mathematics. To find a type of mathematics that gave both order *and* freedom, however, { } had to become a mathematician and examine many different mathematical systems to find a suitable one. Most systems gave too much order; they completely determined the whole future of existence, so that any being governed by such a system would simply be an automaton, and there would be no creativity. { } kept at it, though, and found a type of mathematics that imposed order, but also had the potential for freedom. That freedom, the freedom we have, comes at the end of a series of steps that are as follows:

First, inherent in the mathematics was a relatively simple universe with mathematical "objects" that acted like particles—electrons, neutrinos, and quarks. The quarks could combine to make the protons and neutrons that constitute the nuclei of atoms. Second, from the protons, neutrons, and electrons, elements could be made. These could bind together in molecules that could be very complex.

Third, the complex molecules could be joined together to form organisms, something alive. The organisms had the potential to become more complex by evolving. Each of these organisms would have as its "puppeteer" an intelligent nonphysical Mind, one of the facets of Pure Intelligence. The mathematics— and this is the crucial step—allowed *choices* for the actions and (for more complicated organisms) *thoughts* of the organisms. From the choices presented by the mathematics, the Mind could freely choose the actions of the physical organisms (the puppets). It is the freely choosing Mind associated with the complex arrangements of molecules that makes the organism alive.

As the organisms evolved further, they would come to have nervous systems—onboard computers—to help them make choices. Finally, { } could foresee the possibility in the mathematics that the organisms would evolve into human beings, with nervous systems of such power and potential that they could greatly advance the movement of existence toward the goals of friendship-intimacy and creativity. Further, the human brain-body would enable the Mind that inhabited and directed it to evolve so that many of us could, if we chose, become Great Beings (such as the historical masters, saints, and prophets), worthy lovers, although not remotely the equals, of { }.

THE MYSTIC'S PRACTICES

So far in this chapter, I have summarized the description of our physical world that is given in parts 2 and 3 of the book. Now I will say a little about part 5, where the mystical practices that are designed to transcend the limiting properties of the brain and other aspects of physical existence are given. The goals of those practices are:

- To relax the strong focus of the Mind on what is happening in the brain
- To alter our overall mindset, our view of what reality is like, our view of what is possible and not possible
- To find ways of enhancing perception on the other planes
- To become attuned to and guided by the higher emotions
- To develop the qualities of the self until we each become a Great Being, capable of enhancing the quality of all of existence

What are the ideas behind mystical practices? They are as follows:

- You need to see experientially how mechanistic and not-under-your-conscious-control your thoughts are. And you need to see that there is something in you that is deeper than your brain thoughts and lower emotions.
- You need *reminders* (such as breath or visualization practices) of what exists on the nonphysical planes.
- The habits of the Mind—thinking the physical world is all there is, fear, anger, self-pity—are strengthened by our daily use of them. And so there are practices, done during one's everyday life, to disrupt and weaken these habits.
- There are practices that show us we need not be the captive of our neurochemically related emotions and moods.

- During the course of our lives here, we usually acquire restrictive mindsets, a narrow focus of the Mind, a narrow perspective. There are practices to break this narrow perspective.
- By doing certain practices, we can become aware of what our motivations are and what the motivations behind those motivations are until we come to the highest motivations of all.
- Finally, the practices—necessary though they are—can make us uptight and displeased with ourselves. So we need to keep in mind that a primary goal of the practices is to *relax*—relax our strong focus on the physical, on our restrictive mindsets, on the emotional state of our brain—and simply see existence as it is.

PART 2

PHYSICS

CLASSICAL PHYSICS

Physics is a prime example of modern, analytical, reductive Western thought. It has used each major discovery over its three-hundred-year history as a springboard for further discoveries and has now reached a position where it can explain a wide range of the phenomena of inanimate physical existence. We might think that the reductive aspect of physics, its investigation of phenomena on smaller and smaller scales—atomic, subatomic, quark—would make it more and more remote from the nature of human existence, but that has not proved to be true. What has emerged is a theory of the physical universe that has an astonishing unity. This unity strongly suggests that physics has reached such a fundamental level that it can indeed tell us something essential about the nature of the physical universe, and thereby something essential about the nature of human existence.

GOALS OF THE PHYSICS SECTION

There are three primary goals for the physics part of the book. The first is to show that there is no scientific basis for materialism—the belief that the material component to existence is all that there is. The second is to show that physics and mysticism are compatible by showing that they apply to two distinctly different but intimately interwoven domains, the physical and the nonphysical. And the third, closely linked to the second, is to explain the basic connection between these two domains. To achieve these goals, I will discuss only the bare bones of physics, those parts that bear directly on the question of whether physics allows existence to have a nonphysical component.

Physics as we know it started around 1700 A.D., in a form now called classical physics. Classical physics was superseded by quantum mechanics in 1926. As we will see, classical physics is not compatible with mysticism, while quantum mechanics is.

PHYSICS & MATHEMATICS

One of the keys to understanding the nature of the physical universe lies in an appreciation of the physicist's point of view on mathematics. In both the classical and quantum-mechanics versions of physics, there is a mathematical description of the behavior of the inanimate world. Because the mathematics describes the physical world so well, physicists—myself included—take the mathematical description seriously; we assume that the mathematics accurately portrays actual properties of the physical world. So, much of the physics is an explanation of the insights that can be deduced about the physical world from the mathematics it obeys. Those insights come from the interpretation of the equations of physics.

I hasten to add, however, that physics has another component that is just as important as the mathematics; namely, experiments. These are the ingenious methods devised by physicists to probe more deeply into the nature of matter than our everyday observations ever could. How could you ever tell from everyday observations, for example, that matter is made up of atoms, or that atoms are made up of electrons, protons, and neutrons?

The equations of physics are the distillation of the results of millions of experiments. Thus, because these experiments and the resulting equations give the most penetrating and unified perspective on our universe, nonphysicists must rely on the insights of physics (taken with a grain of commonsense salt) for a deeper understanding of the nature of matter.

CLASSICAL PHYSICS

The equations of classical physics were discovered by Isaac Newton in the latter half of the seventeenth century. In his early twenties, Newton took two years off from his studies to avoid the populous cities where the Black Plague was rampant. During that time he concentrated on the problem of how to describe motion mathematically. To solve it, he had to invent the mathematical discipline of calculus. Using this tool, he formulated three laws of motion which were, and still are, of such great generality that the problem of the motion of matter was completely solved, or, more accurately, completely solved for a large class of problems, a class that includes most of the problems arising in everyday situations.

A BILLIARD-BALL UNIVERSE

MATHEMATICAL DETERMINISM

To appreciate the implications of classical physics, consider a game of billiards. The cue ball is shot and hits a ball, which hits another, and another until all the balls finally stop moving. Classical physics says that once the cue ball is set in motion, the future motion of all the balls can be exactly calculated (taking into account the resistance of the felt, the weight and hardness of the balls, and so on) by using the appropriate equations.

PHYSICAL DETERMINISM

The equations used in the calculation of the motion of the billiard balls will not be exact; there will, for example, be unaccounted-for irregularities in the table and the balls themselves. But the physicist says that, in principle, all these irregularities could be taken into account and the motion calculated exactly. Then, because the physicist puts such faith in the mathematics, he or she says that the mathematics completely determines the motion: *the actual physical motion, once it is started, is completely determined.* Thus there is no freedom in the motion (if classical physics is the paradigm).

PHYSICAL UNIVERSE

The same reasoning can be applied to the whole physical universe. Matter is made up of atoms,[1] and the atoms (in classical physics) can be thought of as tiny billiard balls. Then, as with life-sized billiard balls, once the atoms are set in motion, their future motion is determined forever; the future is completely set. This deterministic view was supported by the many successes of classical physics—the extremely accurate calculation of the motion of the planets, for example, or the calculation of the efficiency of a steam engine.

PARTICLES

Many scientists think of particles—atoms, electrons, neutrons, protons—as being very much like tiny billiard balls. When they collide, for example, they bounce off each other like billiard balls. We will see later, however, that there is no justification for this billiard-ball picture—or any picture—of particles in quantum mechanics. That is, we will see that, despite the heavy emphasis placed on the particle picture of matter in physics, there is no convincing evidence that particles exist; it is quite possible—indeed more likely than the existence of particles—that only the wave function of quantum mechanics exists.

MATERIALISM

The philosophical consequences of the classical billiard-ball universe are (to me) dismal. First, classical physics describes a totally self-sufficient universe; there is no need for God or anything other than the material universe, because classical physics can (or so it seemed before 1900) completely explain the universe. This view—that there is only the physical universe—is materialism.

Many scientists currently still hold this view even though there is no basis for it in modern physics. Why? Primarily because the particle concept has been accepted without serious questioning. In addition, as you will see, it takes some looking beneath the surface to perceive the nonmaterialistic implications of quantum mechanics.

The second philosophical consequence of classical physics follows from the materialistic view that our brains are made up of atoms and our thoughts are composed entirely of the deterministic motions of those atoms. That means that our thoughts and actions are not really free; for because the motion of the atoms is determined, our thoughts and actions are also determined, even though we think we have freedom of choice. This is *determinism,* no free will.

Classically derived determinism and materialism imply there is no non-physical aspect to existence, thus no mysticism. So if mysticism is not to be in conflict with physics, classical physics must not be the full story. And indeed, as we will see in the next chapter, it is not.

Note: There is a summary of the physics in chapter 13. If you do not wish to follow all the physics, you can just read that chapter, plus chapter 12 for its mystical content. If you then want a better understanding of the many-possible-futures idea, read chapter 7.

QUANTUM MECHANICS

As experimental techniques became more advanced during the late 1800s, phenomena were found that could not be explained by classical physics; for example, classical physics could not explain the amount of light given off by the white-hot filament in an incandescent lightbulb. The search for an understanding of this and other phenomena led, over a period of three decades, to quantum mechanics. Quantum mechanics is now universally acknowledged as *the* theory of the physical universe. Classical physics has become a subordinate theory, for its equations follow from the equations of quantum mechanics.

Quantum mechanics involves an enormous conceptual break with classical physics, for the classical particles disappear from the mathematics, and only the wave function (to be explained in a moment), a quantity with no classical analog, appears. Because this conceptual gap is so wide, quantum mechanics was not discovered by a single person, as Newton did with classical mechanics. Instead, the path from classical to quantum theory involved a sequence of insights and experiments, each suggested by a different person. These insights, fueled by a search for a mathematical description of Nature, led to a totally unanticipated theory, a theory in which there is no objective reality and no determinism, a theory in which there are many possible futures.

MANY POSSIBLE FUTURES

In classical physics, equations determine the paths of objects such as billiard balls, baseballs, planets, and atomic particles. The future of the physical universe is completely determined by the mathematics once it is set in motion. That is, there is only one possible future.

Quantum mechanics, however, presents a very different picture; there are *many* futures allowed by its mathematics. This many-possible-futures concept is all-important. It is, in the scheme given here, the mathematical basis of our ability to choose our actions and thoughts (from among the many choices allowed by quantum mechanics). And it is a pointer to a nonphysical component of existence, for we will see that "that which chooses" cannot be part of physical existence. The primary objective of this chapter is to illustrate how quantum mechanics allows many possible futures.

THE WAVE FUNCTION

In classical physics, the electron, as well as every other particle, was thought of as a point particle, an infinitely small billiard ball. All its mass and charge were concentrated at a point. In quantum mechanics, however, the electron (and every other particle) is represented by a wave function. To visualize the wave function, you can think of it as a mist spread out over space. The mist is thick, nearly opaque, in some places, and more transparent in others. (There is an equation in quantum mechanics, the Schrödinger equation, which determines how the mist moves and where it is opaque or transparent.) As an example, when an electron is in an atom,[1] it stays near the nucleus. This is visualized as a mist that is nearly opaque near the nucleus and falls off to complete transparency (no mist) far from the nucleus.

For us, the interesting thing about the wave function is that it can sometimes split into two or more widely separated parts. Each of these parts wends its own way through space, and each produces its own consequences. We see only one of the consequences, however, even though several (mathematically) exist together. To make this idea somewhat less abstract, I will give two illustrations.

AN IMAGINARY LIGHT-BEAM EXPERIMENT

This first illustration does not really happen in Nature, but it uses the familiar image of light in place of the unfamiliar concept of the wave function, so it is easier to follow. To set up the illustration, I will first describe an experiment with light that can actually be done. Then I will explain how the results would change if quantum logic applied.

REAL EXPERIMENT WITH NO QUANTUM LOGIC

In this experiment, a light beam is shot toward a prism. The prism divides the beam so that it goes in two different directions, as in figure 7.1.

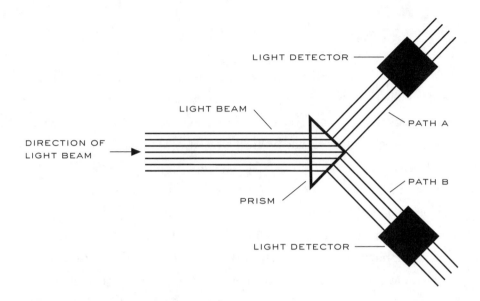

FIGURE 7.1 *A light beam, flowing from left to right, is divided by a prism. The two detectors (square boxes) are filled in in black to show they both detect light in this real (not imaginary) experiment.*

The lines represent the beam of light, and the squares represent detectors of light, with detectors filled in when they have detected light passing through them. Both detectors would register the passage of light in this real experiment, as shown in figure 7.1.

IMAGINARY EXPERIMENT WITH QUANTUM LOGIC

Now turn the light off and suppose "quantum logic" applies. When you turn the light back on, you will not see figure 7.1. Instead, you will see either figure 7.2 or figure 7.3; the light will follow *only one path*. (Remember, this is an illustration; it does not correspond to anything in everyday life, so you cannot make everyday sense out of it.) If you turn the light off and on several times, then the light will take only one path each time, but the path it takes will not always be the same; it will change *at random* from one off-on trial to the next.

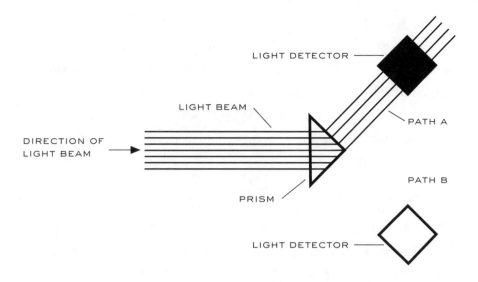

FIGURE 7.2 *The light taking only path A in an imagined result of the light experiment. The filled-in detector detected light while the not-filled-in detector did not.*

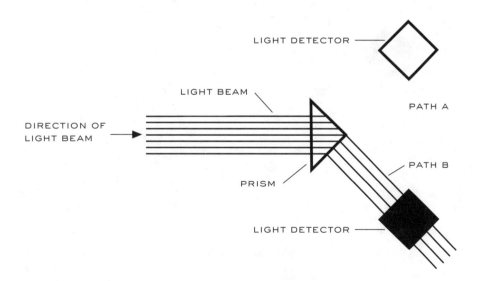

FIGURE 7.3 *The light taking only path B in an imagined result of the light experiment. As in figure 7.2, the filled-in detector detected light while the other did not.*

If we consider the experiment at the time just before the light goes through the prism, the many (two in this case) possible futures are the two possible directions for the light after it goes through the prism. This imaginary experiment illustrates the fact that only one of the possible futures is perceived (the light either goes along the upper path or the lower path, but not both). It also illustrates the randomness that occurs in quantum mechanics.

THE STERN-GERLACH EXPERIMENT

The next illustration, the Stern-Gerlach experiment, is an actual experiment that can be (and has been) performed in a laboratory. In this experiment, where quantum logic actually does apply, an electron is shot into a magnetic field.[2]

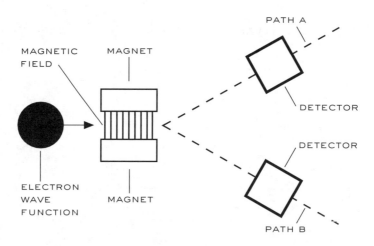

FIGURE 7.4 *An electron wave function about to pass through a magnetic field. The circle represents the wave function, the squares represent detectors, and the dotted lines denote the paths the two parts of the electron wave function will take after it passes through the magnetic field.*

Figure 7.4 is drawn before the electron reaches the magnetic field, with the circle representing the wave function of the electron.

After going through the magnetic field, the wave function divides into two parts, with one part moving up along path A and the other part down along path B, as in figure 7.5. (The reason it splits into two parts is too technical to explain here.)

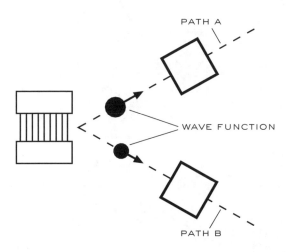

FIGURE 7.5 *After passing through the magnetic filed, the wave function splits into two parts. As indicated by the size, more of the wave function went along path A than path B. (For a more informative rendering of the mathematics, see figure 7.8.)*

The results of the experiment correspond exactly to those of the imaginary light experiment; the electron wave function will either set off the detector on path A, as in figure 7.6, or it will set off the detector on path B, as in figure 7.7, but it will not set off both detectors. (As I will explain later, the different sizes of the A and B wave functions have to do with probability.)

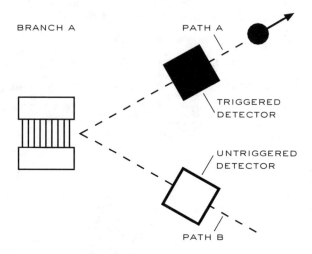

FIGURE 7.6 *Perception of branch A in the Stern-Gerlach experiment.*

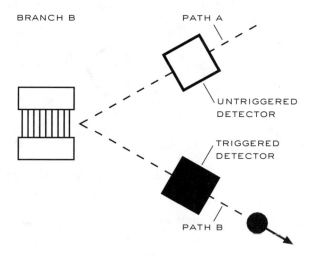

FIGURE 7.7 *Perception of branch B in the Stern-Gerlach experiment.*

If electrons are shot into the apparatus one after another, each one will be detected as taking only one path. As in the light experiment, the path taken will not always be the same; it will change at random from one trial to the next. *The mathematics of quantum mechanics does not predict which path will be taken.* This is the indeterminacy, or randomness, of quantum mechanics.

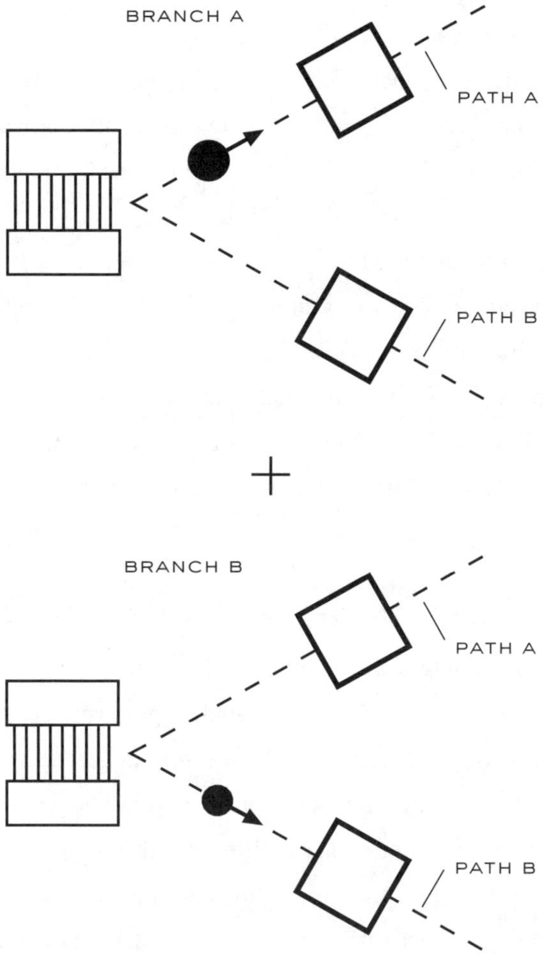

FIGURE 7.8 *To properly illustrate the mathematics, the two parts of the wave function after it splits must be drawn in separate diagrams, as indicated by the + sign, in contrast to figure 7.5. Each diagram represents a branch of the wave function, and the total wave function is the sum of the two branches.*

BRANCHES

Figures 7.6 and 7.7 correctly illustrate the possible perceived results of the Stern-Gerlach experiment, but we are interested in what the wave function is doing between the magnet and the detectors as well as in the results. To explain the wave function's behavior, we must back up to the time just after the electron went through the magnetic field. Figure 7.5 gives the basic idea that the wave function split, but it does not properly represent what happens. To accurately represent the behavior of the wave function, figure 7.5 must be replaced by figure 7.8.

We see that the wave function follows the two paths simultaneously, but it does so in two separate diagrams, almost as if the two paths were two separate events. Each diagram represents one part of the wave function. The two parts are connected by a plus sign in the mathematics of the wave function, so we put a + in the figure. Each different part is called a *branch* of the wave function, because the wave function "branched" into two parts.

PERCEPTION OF ONLY ONE BRANCH

Now as time passes, the two separate diagrams, or branches, evolve independently; the part of the wave function on branch A goes through the A detector, the part on branch B goes through the B detector, and we arrive at figure 7.9.

You can see that tracing the wave function's development does not help explain the perceived results—*either* path A *or* path B—because *both* possible results are present together. Instead, figure 7.9 illustrates one of the primary mysteries of quantum mechanics; two possible outcomes (path A or path B) are simultaneously present in the wave function, but we perceive only one of them (either A or B but not both).

In *any* experiment involving quantum mechanics, the different branches of the wave function correspond to different observable outcomes. It is a general rule of quantum mechanics that *only one of the branches, only one of the possible outcomes, is perceived;* a mixture is never perceived. I will call this rule "only-one perception." The principle that only one branch is perceived cannot be deduced from the mathematics. Instead, it is a statement of how the mathematics is to be brought into agreement with what we see.

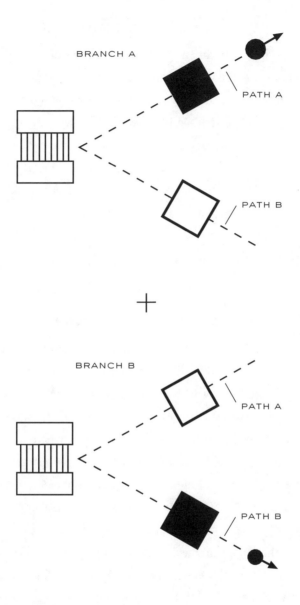

FIGURE 7.9 *A pictorial representation of the two branches of the wave function after the two parts have passed through their respective detectors. The triggered detectors are shown in black. The two branches f the wave function represent the two possible outcomes of the experiment (figures 7.6 and 7.7).*

TWO OUTCOMES

In the Stern-Gerlach experiment, there are two possible outcomes. I will describe these not using the word *electron,* because I will argue later that there is no good reason to believe that electrons exist. Either the A detector is triggered or the B detector is triggered. Or, if we look at the experiment at the time just before the wave function goes through the magnet, we can say there are two possible futures; either the A detector will be triggered or the B detector will be triggered. There is no way of deducing from the mathematics which possibility will become reality. This is the indeterminacy of quantum mechanics; it presents a choice of futures (path A or path B) but it does not determine which one will become the future that is perceived.

OBJECTIVE REALITY?

What does the Stern-Gerlach experiment tell us? It tells us that once the electron wave function splits, physical existence—if we take the mathematics of quantum mechanics seriously, and we do—*splits into two separate realities!* There is one reality, corresponding to branch A, where the wave function triggers the A but not the B detector, and another reality where the wave function triggers the B but not the A detector. *There is no longer a single objective reality* (at least in the mathematics); there are two versions of reality, with each branch representing one version. (In more complicated examples, there can be more than two branches, hence more than two versions of reality.)

So we see that quantum mechanics is a radical theory—no objective reality! But in everyday life we all perceive and agree on a single reality, as if there were indeed an objective reality. How, then, is our experience to be reconciled with quantum mechanics? The way physicists normally deal with this is to say that the wave function is not the physical reality; it is only describing an actual, single, underlying, objectively existing physical reality.

Quantum mechanics didn't come with an instruction manual when it was discovered, however, and so there is no guarantee that the "underlying objectively existing reality" view is correct. Thus we are free to assume, in our search for a way in which physics and mysticism can be fit together, that there is no underlying objectively existing physical reality.

But if quantum mechanics allows two results—two realities—in the Stern-Gerlach experiment, I must still explain why we all see the same result; that is, if there is no objective reality, why can't I see path A and you see path B as the result? The answer lies partly in an assumption and partly in the mathematics. The assumption is that of only-one perception; (for unknown reasons) we each see only one branch of the wave function. Having made this assumption, the mathematics *then* tells us that two people can never disagree on the readings of the detectors; that is, they can never disagree on which branch constitutes "reality." Thus, when observing the outer world (rather than the inner world of thought; see chapter 10), there is an effective objective reality, a reality on which we all agree.

THE PROBABILITY LAW

There is one more principle of quantum mechanics illustrated by the Stern-Gerlach experiment. In figure 7.9, we have drawn the circle corresponding to the branch A wave function larger than the circle corresponding to the branch B wave function. Suppose that two-thirds of the wave function goes along path A and one-third goes along path B (the amount that goes along each path is determined by the mathematics). If we repeat the experiment many times and keep all the conditions the same, the path A detector will be triggered two-thirds of the time and the path B detector, one-third. This is the probability law of quantum mechanics. We do not know why this law holds.

Choosing. The mathematics of quantum mechanics does not tell us whether we will perceive branch A or branch B in the Stern-Gerlach experiment. In fact, nothing is known in physics about how the single perceived branch is chosen from among the possible branches.

REVIEW

- Instead of dealing with particles and the paths they take, as classical physics does, quantum mechanics deals with the wave function. This may be pictured as a mist, nearly opaque (thick mist) in some places and nearly transparent (no mist) in others.

- The laws of quantum mechanics tell us that under certain conditions, the wave function will divide into two or more widely separated parts or branches, each with its own consequences. Each of these branches represents a *potential future*. See figure 7.9 for an example.

- Each branch corresponds to a potential version of reality. For reasons unknown to science, only one branch is perceived (only-one perception); that is, only one of the potential futures becomes the actual perceived present.

- Quantum mechanics does not tell us which potential version of reality will be the one we see. Thus quantum mechanics does not determine the future; it is an indeterminate theory.

MACROSCOPIC & MICROSCOPIC— SCHRÖDINGER'S CAT

We have seen that the mathematics of quantum mechanics allows many possible futures. Before we can make use of this idea, however, we must consider the following problem: Quantum mechanics is relevant only on the atomic scale, but human life is lived on a scale a hundred million times larger than that. How, then, can quantum mechanics be relevant to us? To see how, we must consider the idea of scale in more detail.

MACROSCOPIC DETERMINISM, MICROSCOPIC CHOICE

There is an absolute length scale in the physical world corresponding to the size of an atom, and for that reason I will occasionally use the diameter of a hydrogen atom as a unit of length. (About 100 million atoms fit into a one-centimeter length.) If the scale is large—if we are talking about a golf ball, for example—then there will be only one branch to the wave function, and quantum mechanics reduces to classical physics. If the scale is small, though, then there can be many branches to the wave function, and thus many possible futures. The dividing line between large scale—macroscopic—and small scale—microscopic—is around one thousand atoms, or one-thousandth the diameter of a human hair. A tennis ball bouncing off the ground is a deterministic macroscopic event with only one possible outcome, while the collision of two atoms is an indeterminate microscopic event in which there is more than one possible outcome.

THE BEGINNING OF A MACROSCOPIC EVENT

It can happen, however—and this is the point of this chapter—that both microscopic and macroscopic scales are involved in the same event; the *beginning* of a macroscopic event can be dependent upon a microscopic event. In that case, each different microscopic possibility at the beginning can lead to a different macroscopic event at the end. And so, even though each macroscopic event itself is deterministic, the initial choice of *which* macroscopic event occurs is not deterministic.

We have already seen this microscopic-macroscopic coupling in the Stern-Gerlach experiment. The microscopic event is the electron wave function going through the magnetic field and splitting into two branches. The two possible macroscopic results are the A detector being activated or the B detector being activated.

SCHRÖDINGER'S CAT

There is another well-known example in which microscopic choice leads to different deterministic macroscopic results, and that is Schrödinger's cat.

(This is a gedankenexperiment, an experiment done in one's imagination—in this case, that of Austrian physicist Erwin Schrödinger, 1887–1961.) In Schrödinger's experiment, a cat is placed in a sealed box along with a Geiger counter (radiation detector), atoms undergoing nuclear decay, and a vial of cyanide. In nuclear decay, which is a microscopic event, a neutron in the atom's nucleus decays (splits) into a proton, an electron, and a neutrino. When that happens, the wave function of the nucleus splits. Quantum mechanics tells us that a given nucleus will have a wave function that is a combination of two parts, or branches. On one branch, the wave function is split, and on the other branch, it is not split. So the two branches of the wave function are "split" and "not split."

The two branches of the wave function include not only the nucleus, but also the Geiger counter, the cyanide, and the cat. On the "split" branch, the Geiger counter detects the nuclear decay, sends a signal that breaks the vial of cyanide, and the cat dies. On the "not-split" branch, the Geiger counter sends no signal and the cat lives. The two branches—ending with cat alive or cat dead—are each deterministic once the Geiger counter registers or does not register a decay. But the two very different macroscopic results—cat alive or cat dead—depend on a single, indeterminate, microscopic event (the decay of a nucleus).

THE BRAIN-BODY, DETERMINISM & CHOICE

Schrödinger's cat is a graphic example of how microscopic events can influence macroscopic events. Does this idea have anything to do with our everyday, human lives? Yes, it does. Most of the body's processes—contraction of muscles, transmission of nerve signals—are macroscopically deterministic. In the brain, however, there are junctions called synapses between nerve cells. These are small enough so that quantum mechanics, with its resultant indeterminacy, applies; the synapse wave function can have different branches.

The synapses are crucial elements of the brain because they help to control the flow of thoughts. In fact, it turns out that we can control the flow of thoughts and what actions we take by controlling which branch of the synapse wave function becomes the effective reality. (More detail is given in chapters 11 and 15.) The actions of the body, once initiated, are still macroscopically deterministic, but by choosing at the microscopic synaptic level, we can choose which deterministic action to take, which thought to think.

REVIEW

- Large-scale events are deterministic, but events on the atomic scale are indeterminate because quantum mechanics applies. Our bodies are large scale, so why should the indeterminacy of quantum mechanics be relevant? It is relevant because atomic-scale events at the synapses of the brain can determine *which* large-scale (deterministic) events occur.

- Example of Schrödinger's cat. The atomic-scale indeterminate event is the decay of a nucleus, with the indeterminacy being decay or non-decay. If the nucleus does not decay, the cat lives; but if it does decay, the cat dies. So the indeterminate atomic-scale event determines which large-scale event occurs.

- An analogous thing happens in the brain. The atomic-scale events are what happen at the synapses of the brain. The large-scale events are the firings of neurons, which determine our thoughts. Thus, the quantum choices at the synapses—and I will indicate later that we do indeed have a say in the choice—determine which thought we think.

WAVES VERSUS PARTICLES—
THE WAVE PICTURE

If particles exist, then their motion is almost certainly deterministic, and it is virtually certain that no nonphysical agent could affect their motion. So, if I want to find a link between physics and a mysticism that is relevant for life on earth, then I need to show there is no convincing evidence that particles exist. That is what I will do in this chapter. (It would be better if I could prove that particles don't exist, but I don't see how to do that at this time.)

The same insights needed to show there is no evidence for particles also lay the foundation for distinguishing between the physical and nonphysical aspects of existence, and for understanding the connection between them. In addition, no evidence for particles means there is no evidence for materialism in physics.

INTERPRETATIONS OF QUANTUM MECHANICS

Quantum mechanics proper consists of two parts. First, there are the equations for the wave function. Second, physicists must deal with the fact that the wave function allows many possible futures instead of just the one we see. This is done first by simply declaring that only one branch of the wave function is perceived and second by stipulating that the probability for the perception of different branches depends on the wave function in such and such a way (the details are irrelevant).

But there is also a third part to quantum mechanics which, in contrast to the first two, has no bearing on our ability to describe physical reality mathematically. The third part, called an *interpretation* of quantum mechanics, provides *a mental picture that explains why only one branch is perceived.* The mental picture is a valid interpretation, of course, only if it does not violate any of the established principles of quantum mechanics. There is currently more than one valid interpretation.

THE PARTICLE INTERPRETATION

The most common interpretation is that particles—electrons, protons, atoms—objectively exist. In the Stern-Gerlach experiment, for example, where an electron wave function passes through and is split by a magnetic field, the particle interpretation says there is an actual electron that travels on one branch or the other. If the electron travels on the path A, then we will see the A detector registering the passage of the electron; if it travels on path B, the B detector will register its passage. More generally, a particle will travel on only one branch, and it is the traveled-upon branch that is perceived.

The question is whether there is any solid evidence for the particle interpretation. I will consider all the main arguments used to justify the particle concept and show that none of them is convincing.

ARGUMENTS FOR & AGAINST
THE PARTICLE INTERPRETATION

I. HISTORICAL CONSIDERATIONS

The particle concept has been used in physics for three hundred years with great success, so physicists are understandably reluctant to give it up. *Counterargument:* There is no doubt that a particlelike model for matter is extremely useful, but that does not show that particles exist. For one can show that the properties of the wave function alone, without the presumed existence of particles, can account for the particlelike properties that are so useful.

2. PERCEPTION OF ONLY ONE BRANCH

One might cite the perception of only one branch—only-one perception—as evidence that particles exist. How else are we to explain why only one branch is perceived? *Counterargument:* The existence of particles that travel on only one branch of the wave function would indeed explain why only one branch is perceived, but there may well be other explanations of only-one perception. Unless independent evidence—evidence independent of only-one perception—is found that shows unequivocally that particles exist and are the cause of only-one perception, we must conclude that the cause of only-one perception is unknown.

3. PARTICLELIKE PROPERTIES

There are certain properties that are ascribed to particles in both classical physics and quantum mechanics. These are mass, energy, momentum, angular momentum (spin), and charge (you need not fully understand these terms). These properties are the most basic and universally used quantities in physics; they, plus the property of localization, *define* the concept of a particle.

These particlelike properties *appear* to be carried by objectively existing particles. An electron (or electronlike wave function), for example, has a definite amount of mass and electrical charge, so physicists conjecture there is a lump of matter, existing in space and time, that carries the mass and charge. *Counterargument:* The counterargument here is technical, so you may not be able to follow it fully. Nevertheless, you can get the gist of it.

The equations of quantum mechanics are linear and relativistically invariant (don't panic; you need not understand). This implies that the mathematical discipline of group representation theory can be applied. The result is a proof that mass, energy, momentum, and angular momentum (spin) are unequivocally properties of the wave function. That is, it is a mathematical fact that *these particlelike properties will exist as properties of the wave function and have all their usual characteristics and consequences, even if particles don't exist.*[1]

Group theoretic reasoning can also be used in conjunction with the internal symmetry group (symmetries not related to space and time) to show that charge, too, is a property of the wave function and exists whether particles exist or not.

Thus, incredibly, the properties used to *define* the concept of a particle turn out to be—beyond doubt—properties of the *wave function!* This strongly suggests that it is the wave function, rather than particles, that physically exists. (Conceivably, there could also be particles, in addition to the wave function, that have the same properties, but there is no evidence that this duplication of properties is necessary.)

4. LOCALIZATION

There are experiments in which the wave function is spread out but the effect of the wave function is localized (confined to a small area). This has been interpreted to mean there is a localized particle hidden within the wave function, but there is no evidence that this explanation is correct. Because the argument is more detailed than the others, I have put it in appendix A. An example of localization is given there.

5. THE BELL-ASPECT RESULT

In 1964 the English physicist John Bell[2] was trying to find a way to test whether particles actually existed. He found that if he assumed the influence

of particles was localized—that a measurement of, say, the speed of one particle at one place could not affect the measurement of the speed of another particle ten meters away—then the predictions of quantum mechanics could be
shown to be wrong. Alain Aspect found a way to test this experimentally in
1982. The results were that a measurement at one place *could* affect a measurement at another place. Thus, quantum mechanics was vindicated, but the
(localized) particle concept was not. This is a strong argument in favor of only
the wave function existing.

This experimental result has been interpreted in the popular literature as
showing that everything is connected to everything else, which is said to
imply mysticism. It's nice to have allies, but that is the wrong conclusion to
draw from the experiment, because it is based on the idea that particles—with
instantaneous long-range interactions—exist. The proper conclusion—in my
opinion—is that localized particles don't exist.

6. THE EQUATIONS OF QUANTUM MECHANICS

There is one more important argument in the debate over the existence or
nonexistence of particles. Quantum mechanics is an extremely successful
theory. There are no known instances where it contradicts observation, and
its range of successful applications is enormous (see appendix B). All these
successes rest on the equations of quantum mechanics. And all these equations are *equations for the wave function only*. Thus, the mathematics of quantum mechanics, by itself, confirms the existence of the wave function, but it
gives no hint that particles exist, and it does not need them to exist for its
predictions.

NO PARTICLES

The net result of these deliberations is that there is no convincing evidence
that particles exist. In fact, the third, fifth, and sixth arguments definitely favor
the existence of the wave function alone.[3]

We are therefore free to assume, in our efforts to show that physics and mysticism are compatible, that particles—electrons, protons, atoms—do not exist. (Remember, our goal is not to *prove* that mysticism is correct but to show that there is an interpretation of quantum mechanics that is compatible with mysticism [and with free will], and that this interpretation is at least as reasonable and likely as any other.)

The lack of evidence for objectively existing "material" particles is also important for our purposes because it means there is no support for materialism in physics.

WAVE-PARTICLE DUALITY

One of the seeming paradoxes of modern physics is that sometimes—when there are interference effects, for example, as occur with light—matter seems to behave like a wave. And sometimes—when there is localization, for example, or when energy and momentum are involved—matter seems to behave like a particle. My resolution of the wave-particle paradox is to suppose that there are only waves (the wave function), and that—as has been shown—the particlelike properties of the waves account for the particlelike behavior of matter. In other words, the "material" that makes up our physical world consists of particlelike wave functions rather than of particles.

THE COLLAPSE INTERPRETATION

When I said before that there was no objective reality, I implicitly assumed that all branches of the wave function continued forever. However, there have been attempts to make quantum mechanics compatible with objective reality by assuming that the wave function collapses down to just one branch (which becomes the objective reality).

One of the early interpretations of quantum mechanics was the wave collapse or wave reduction hypothesis of John Von Neumann (1903–1957). He proposed that at certain instants the wave function collapsed down from many branches to only one branch. He gave no reason for this collapse and named no mechanism that caused it. He simply assumed that, at certain instants, the mathematics of quantum mechanics ceased to hold and the wave function collapsed. That is, he assumed that the mathematics of quantum mechanics was, at certain times, countermanded, overruled.

More recently, collapse schemes with mathematical mechanisms have been proposed,[4] but there is no evidence for them and they run into stiff technical difficulties. Thus, collapse of the wave function cannot be considered to be a viable interpretation of quantum mechanics at this time.

In addition to mathematical mechanisms of collapse, some scientists have proposed schemes in which the (nonphysical) Mind collapses the wave function. I do not think these proposals are viable because they call for suspension of the mathematics of quantum mechanics at certain times, and that seems untenable. They run into the same problem raised by critics of Descartes' dualism—how can something nonphysical affect the physical? (Rene Descartes [1596–1660], a French mathematician and philosopher, was one of the earliest Europeans to suggest that existence splits into two distinct parts, physical and nonphysical.) Our scheme gets around this objection to dualism by assuming that the Mind chooses; it singles out one branch to concentrate on, but does not alter the wave function in any way.

The net result is that there is no reason to assume that any of the branches of the wave function ever cease to exist.

THE WAVE PICTURE

As I said earlier, there are several different interpretations of quantum mechanics, none of which violate any physical principle. I will choose one that is compatible both with free choice of our actions and thoughts, and also with mysticism. To this end, I will assume—as has been justified previously—that there are no particles and that all branches of the wave function continue forever. This is what I call the wave picture.

It is worth emphasizing the status of the wave picture; it is simply a statement of the content of the mathematics of quantum mechanics as it now stands. It is not yet an interpretation because there is no explanation of only-one perception, but it will become the basis for the Mind interpretation in the next chapter.

THE PHYSICAL UNIVERSE

In this book, I make a sharp distinction between the physical and nonphysical parts of existence. To this end, I will *define* the physical universe as consisting of the wave function and the wave function alone. All else in existence belongs to the nonphysical aspect of existence. Why this particular division? Because as far as we know, quantum mechanics gives an all-encompassing theory of the physical universe, and nothing "exists" in (the mathematics of) quantum mechanics except the wave function. And because, as far as we know, the wave function is a neatly self-contained universe; nothing outside the wave function can influence the wave function.

One might argue that our knowledge is not complete; something—the Mind, say—might be able to alter the wave function and therefore ought to be considered as part of the physical universe. That could conceivably be, but one of our "rules" here is that we work from science *as it currently is*. Otherwise we are considering ungrounded, speculative ideas that almost certainly will not add to our insight.

REVIEW

- An interpretation of quantum mechanics provides a mental picture
  of why only one branch of the wave function is perceived.

- The most common interpretation is that particles objectively exist. If this interpretation is correct, then there is no nonphysical component to existence, and thus no mysticism. And we have no free choice of our actions and thoughts.

- The two most persuasive arguments that particles exist are first that there must be something to carry the mass and charge of, for example, an electron, and second that the reason a spread-out wave function produces a localized effect is because there is an actually existing particle hidden within the wave function. Neither argument provides convincing evidence that particles exist, because the properties of the wave function alone can account for these properties. Thus, we are free to assume (although we have not proven) that particles do not exist—that is, that there are no objectively existing electrons or atoms.

- There is no reason to believe that the mathematics of quantum mechanics ever ceases to apply. This implies that there is no reason to believe that any of the branches of the wave function ever cease to exist.

- These last two points are the basis for our wave picture of quantum mechanics. In this picture, there are no particles, and all branches of the wave function continue forever. This picture provides the basis for the Mind interpretation of quantum mechanics given in the next chapter, with that interpretation providing the connection between the physical and nonphysical worlds.

QUANTUM MECHANICS &
THE NONPHYSICAL MIND

In the last chapter, I assumed the wave picture of reality holds; physical reality is made up solely of the wave function, with all its branches. But I didn't explain why we perceive a single reality when many (all the different branches) exist. To explain that single reality, we are forced to assume that there is more to existence than the physical world. For each of us, this additional part of reality takes the form of a nonphysical Mind.

NO PERCEPTION OF ONLY ONE BRANCH
WITHIN QUANTUM MECHANICS

To see the need for a nonphysical component of reality, we will return to the Stern-Gerlach experiment. I will again draw the two branches of the wave function as in figure 7.9, but this time I will include an observer—a person observing the readings of the meters—with the observer represented in the diagram, figure 10.1, by a drawing of a brain.

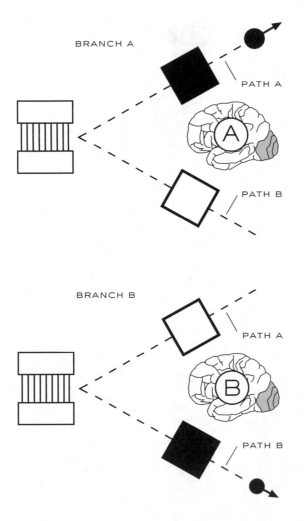

FIGURE 10.1 *This is Figure 7.9 redrawn with an observer, represented by the brain, perceiving the results of the Stern-Gerlach experiment. There is no longer "an" observer. Instead there are two "versions" of an observer, one perceiving path A and one perceiving path B, as indicated by the letters superimposed on the brain.*

This figure shows that a most peculiar state of affairs occurs in quantum mechanics. The brain on branch A will see the meters registering path A while the brain on branch B will see the meters registering path B. Thus, there is no longer a single objectively existing brain; instead there are two copies of the brain, one seeing path A and the other seeing path B! No objective reality in quantum mechanics! Imagine that the observer is you. Which copy is the real you? How does it come about that only one copy of your brain is consciously aware of what it sees?

If a physicist were to accept the wave picture but still wish to cling to materialism, he would say that the place to look for an answer to this question is in a new form of materialism. That is, he would try to find an answer under the assumption that the wave function (rather than particles) is the "material" of existence, and all there is in existence is the wave function. But that assumption does not yield an explanation of why there is only one conscious version, as the following argument shows. (You may skip to step 6 if you do not wish to follow the details of this argument.)

1. There is a law of quantum mechanics which states that each branch is absolutely isolated from each other branch, so there can be no communication between them; there can be no electrical or light or sound signal passed from one to the other, for example.

2. The electron wave function can carry no consciousness-distinguishing feature, no feature that says, "This branch is the one that will be consciously perceived." (To assume otherwise is to go outside conventional quantum mechanics.)

3. There must be some consciousness-distinguishing feature that occurs in the wave function of the brain; that is, some shape or configuration of the wave function must distinguish the "aware" copy of the brain from the other copy.

4. Because the electron wave function carries no consciousness-related information, the consciousness-distinguishing feature must arise within

the wave function of one and only one copy of the brain. However, because there is no communication between branches, the occurrence of the consciousness-distinguishing feature of the two branches cannot be coordinated.

5. This implies that there is no way to guarantee that one and only one branch will be perceived, for both copies could have a "yes" consciousness-distinguishing feature (in which case both would be consciously perceived[1]) or both could have a "no" (in which case neither would be consciously perceived).

6. The net result is that there is no consistent way to perceive one and only one branch if existence consists exclusively of the wave function. Existence, therefore, cannot consist of the wave function alone.

THE NONPHYSICAL MIND

We see, then, that we *must* step outside quantum mechanics for an explanation of only-one perception in the wave picture. (Remember that the wave picture is rigorously implied if one assumes—and there is no argument to the contrary—that the current laws of quantum mechanics need no supplementing.) The only way to do this is to suppose there is a nonquantum mechanical aspect of each of us that perceives all the branches and can concentrate its attention on just one of them.[2] It is the one branch that is concentrated on that becomes the content of ordinary consciousness.

The aspect that concentrates on, and therefore effectively perceives, only one branch must be outside of quantum mechanics (because, as I have shown, it is not possible to consistently single out one and only one branch within quantum mechanics). Therefore, because we define the physical universe as consisting of the wave function alone (because the wave function is what quantum mechanics, the eminently successful theory of the physical universe, applies to), the perceiving aspect must be *nonphysical*. We call this nonphysical aspect the Mind, with each of us having his or her own individual Mind. (The nonphysical "Mind" is capitalized to distinguish it from our ordinary use of the word *mind,* which normally refers to the workings of the physical brain.) It is the nonphysical Mind—that aspect which "looks down from outside" on the wave function—that is the real you.

To summarize, the unadorned theory of quantum mechanics, in conjunction with our perception of only one branch of the wave function, implies that we each harbor a nonphysical aspect—our Mind.

INDIVIDUAL MINDS—
THE MIND PERCEIVES ONLY THE BRAIN

Each of us is presumed to have his or her own individual Mind. What does that Mind perceive? If I assumed that each Mind perceived the wave function of the whole universe, there would be inconsistencies and contradictions in our scheme. To avoid these, I assume that the individual Mind perceives only the wave function of the individual brain. (Actually, the Mind is also no doubt aware of the separate nervous system we have in the digestive system—hence gut feeling—and perhaps other bodily processes also. To keep things simple, though, I will suppose the Mind perceives only the state of the brain.) My Mind perceives the wave function of my brain and your Mind perceives the wave function of your brain. (*Note:* There is a single wave function for any one brain—hence function, not functions—but it is compounded from the wave functions of the many atoms and particles that make up the brain.) So the (brain) wave function is the "substance" of physical existence, and the Mind perceives that substance.

How, then, do we perceive the outer world? We perceive it indirectly through the effect of the outside world on the wave function of each individual brain. The light from a falling leaf enters my eye, my eye sends neural pulses to my brain, and those pulses alter the wave function of my brain. My Mind then perceives the resultant alteration of my brain's wave function and inter-prets it as a leaf falling in the outer world.

THE MIND INTERPRETATION

All these results, taken together, constitute the Mind interpretation of quantum mechanics. First, I assume there are no particles and that physical existence consists solely of the wave function. Second, I assume all the branches of the wave function continue forever. Third, it then follows that there must be a non-physical perceiver of the wave function—the Mind—that perceives only one branch. Finally, each of us has an individual Mind in this interpretation, and each Mind perceives only the wave function of its associated individual brain.

DISADVANTAGES OF THE MIND INTERPRETATION

There are three disadvantages to this proposed interpretation. First, just as there is no experimental evidence for the particle interpretation, there is also no experimental evidence that proves, beyond doubt, that this interpretation is correct. Second, there is no explanation of the probability law (the probability of a branch is related to the "size" of the branch's wave function). And last, be-cause this interpretation requires a nonphysical Mind, it has the disadvantage (to a physicist) that one must conceptually step outside the physical universe to fully understand the quantum mechanical theory of the physical universe.

REASONS FOR CHOOSING
THE MIND INTERPRETATION

THE "INEVITABILITY" OF THE MIND INTERPRETATION

We assume that only the wave function physically exists and that all branches continue forever. If one grants these two assumptions—and there is no evidence against them—then the Mind interpretation is the only possible interpretation.

FREE WILL

The second reason for choosing the Mind interpretation follows from the requirement that an interpretation—without violating any scientific principle—should allow us the freedom to choose our actions and thoughts. (Note that I am simply *assuming* we have free will; it is not possible to show we have free will by purely rational arguments.) The Mind interpretation is ideally suited for this requirement; the freedom comes (as we will elaborate upon in a moment) in the *choice* of which branch of the brain wave function to perceive and thereby bring into our ordinary consciousness.

COMPATIBILITY WITH MYSTICISM

The third reason follows from my requirement that an interpretation—without violating any scientific principle—should be compatible with the mystical view that there is a nonphysical aspect to existence. The Mind interpretation, with its nonphysical Mind, is ideally suited for this second nonphysics requirement also. *The Mind interpretation is*, in fact, *the bridge between physics and mysticism.*

THE PERCEIVING MIND ALSO CHOOSES

In this scheme, there are many branches of the brain wave function, with each branch corresponding to a potential thought or action. I will suppose that the Mind perceives—in a way that is different from our ordinary perception—all the branches. Then the Mind freely chooses which one to focus on, and that chosen one becomes the content of our ordinary consciousness. So the perceiver is also the chooser.

Note, however, that the individual Mind can choose only from internal or brain events—what thought to think, what bodily action to initiate. It cannot choose the course of events when the branching of the wave function occurs outside the brain; it cannot, for example, choose whether to see branch A or branch B in the Stern-Gerlach experiment, or whether to see Schrödinger's cat dead or alive.

PHYSICS & THE NONPHYSICAL

Quantum mechanics, through the Mind interpretation, contains within it a bridge between the physical and the nonphysical. It shows that the physical and nonphysical are compatible. And because the nonphysical Mind chooses our actions and thoughts, it shows that the nonphysical aspect of each of us is a vital part of our existence.

What is physical and what is nonphysical in our everyday lives? Obviously, the world around us is physical, but so also are most of our thoughts and emotions; they correspond to neural firing patterns in our physical brain.

On the other hand, our conscious *choice* of thoughts and actions is nonphysical. There is also a nonphysical component to thoughts themselves, although we are not usually aware of it. (To say that thoughts are both physical and nonphysical may seem confusing. It is. Part of a mystic's training is to sort out the physical aspects from the nonphysical.) And there is a nonphysical component to our emotions.

Intuition is nonphysical. So are some forms of love (or all forms of love, but to greater and lesser degrees). And our entire existence after death is nonphysical.

PHYSICS & METAPHYSICS

We have deduced from quantum mechanics (under certain assumptions) that there is a nonphysical component to existence. The idea that quantum mechanics is the final theory of the physical universe, and is therefore a sound basis for such a deduction, is defended in appendix B.[3] But even though the defense is strong, in light of the not-*absolute*-certainty of the laws of physics, we might ask whether basing metaphysics on physics, at least in part, is a worthwhile endeavor.

In answer, I would say that what we want is deep knowledge of our human nature and there are only four sources upon which to base our search for that knowledge: science; reasoning not based on science; the experience of others, including books and teachers; and our own experience. All four have strengths and weaknesses.

When we look at the historical record over the past few centuries, the conjecture that the basics of quantum mechanics will never be substantially modified or superseded may seem foolish. Nevertheless, because so much of the physical world is accurately described by quantum mechanics in such a consistent and unified way, the argument is convincing. I do not feel that the unlikely chance that quantum mechanics is wrong in its essence makes it any less reliable a guide than reasoning, which depends on our hypotheses; the experience of others, where we must choose whose experience to accept; or even our own experience, for we are all subject to false evaluations of our own experience.

We can never have absolute certainty in our search for deep knowledge and to insist on it will lead to paralysis in our spiritual quest. We are forced to proceed pragmatically by using the first three sources—science, reasoning not based on science, and the experience of others—in as intelligent a manner as possible, as guides to the true experiential knowledge we seek. In this pragmatic framework, the mature science of physics, intensely developed over the past three hundred years, and always subject to the unforgiving test of experiment, offers much valuable insight.

REVIEW

- If all that physically exists is the wave function with its many branches, then perception of only one branch must be due to the *process* of perception.
- In the Mind interpretation, each individual possesses his or her own Mind, with the Mind being responsible for only-one perception. This Mind perceives only the wave function of the individual's own brain.

The Mind cannot be part of the wave function and thus it must be outside the physical universe, that is, nonphysical.

- The nonphysical Mind is the most essential part of the self.
- The Mind interpretation, which violates no physical principle, shows that quantum mechanics is compatible with there being a nonphysical component to existence. And it gives the connection—the nonphysical Mind perceiving the physical wave function of the brain—between the physical and nonphysical realms.
- The Mind interpretation sharply divides existence into a physical and a nonphysical part. Ordinary thoughts and emotions are in the *physical* realm because they correspond to firing patterns of neurons. But the *choice* of thoughts and physical actions, the experience of deeper emotions, and intuition are in the nonphysical realm.

11

THE BRAIN & THE MIND

In the last chapter, I assumed that the Mind perceived the wave function of the brain. In this chapter, I will explore the relation between the nonphysical Mind and the brain in more detail. This will allow us to see the origin of freedom of choice. And it will show us the basics of our personal link between the physical and nonphysical planes of existence.

When you are exposed to ideas for the first time, it is better if you see a less complicated version; otherwise the mind gets overloaded and you don't absorb the material. For this reason, the core of the brain-Mind ideas is presented here while embellishments, ramifications, justifications, and clarifications are given in appendix C.

BRANCHES & THOUGHTS

NEURAL FIRING PATTERNS & THOUGHTS

The brain is made up of billions of neurons (see figure 16.1). Each neuron has the possibility of firing, which means an electrochemical pulse travels from one end of the neuron to the other. Each of our thoughts, neuroscientists tell us, corresponds to a particular pattern of firing neurons. There will be millions of neurons firing for each thought, but to represent this correspondence between thoughts and firing patterns pictorially, we will suppose the brain has only nine neurons (as it does on bad days). Then the neural firing patterns for three different thoughts—say, visualizing a tree, initiating a deep breath, and being aware of what your fingers are feeling—might be as in figure 11.1, with the solid circles representing firing neurons and the open circles representing nonfiring neurons.

VISUALIZING
A TREE

INITIATING A
DEEP BREATH

AWARENESS
OF FINGERS

FIGURE 11.1 *Neural patterns associated with three thoughts. Solid circles represent firing neurons and open circles nonfiring neurons.*

WAVE FUNCTIONS & NEURAL FIRING PATTERNS

To bring quantum mechanics into the picture, I will switch from firing and nonfiring neurons to the wave functions for those neurons. There is one wave function associated with a firing neuron and a different wave function associated with a nonfiring neuron. These are represented by a dark circle and a light circle, respectively, as in figure 11.2.

FIRING NEURON   NONFIRING NEURON

FIGURE 11.2 *Schematic representation of the wave functions associated with firing (dark) and nonfiring (light) neurons.*

We can then put these symbols together to form the wave functions associated with thoughts, as in figure 11.3, taking into account the firing patterns in figure 11.1.

VISUALIZING   INITIATING A   AWARENESS
A TREE   DEEP BREATH   OF FINGERS

FIGURE 11.3 *Wave functions associated with three thoughts. The neural firing patterns of figure 11.1 were used, along with the firing-nonfiring wave functions of figure 11.2.*

In normal awareness, when we think these three thoughts, we don't think them simultaneously; we think them one after the other, although the time difference between them may be only hundredths of a second. What I am proposing is that these three wave functions, corresponding to three thoughts, occur simultaneously in the brain wave function, as is shown in figure 11.4. Each of the three is a branch of the brain wave function.

VISUALIZING
A TREE

INITIATING A
DEEP BREATH

AWARENESS
OF FINGERS

FIGURE 11.4 *The brain wave function with three simultaneous potential thoughts.*

The + signs appear because the brain wave function is the mathematical sum of these three branches.

AWARENESS OF ONLY ONE THOUGHT

Even though the three branches representing thoughts are present in the wave function simultaneously, we are aware (in the normal sense) of only one of them at a time. How do we get from figure 11.4 to that single thought?

The first step is that the Mind, in an instant of time, perceives all three potential thoughts at once, as depicted in figure 11.5.

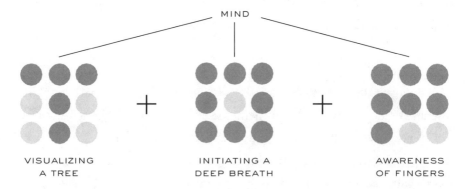

VISUALIZING
A TREE

INITIATING A
DEEP BREATH

AWARENESS
OF FINGERS

FIGURE 11.5 *The mind perceiving three thoughts simultaneously. The Mind's simultaneous awareness is different from ordinary awareness.*

The Mind then chooses one of those thoughts to concentrate on,[1] as is depicted in figure 11.6, and it is that single thought which becomes the content of ordinary consciousness. It is important to note that the Mind has the *freedom to choose* any one of the potential thoughts.

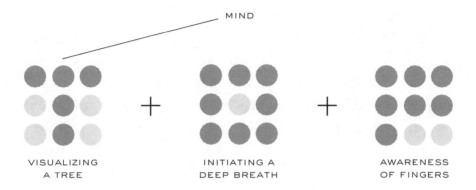

MIND

VISUALIZING
A TREE

INITIATING A
DEEP BREATH

AWARENESS
OF FINGERS

FIGURE 11.6 *The Mind concentrating on one thought. This diagram would correspond to visualizing a tree with ordinary consciousness.*

This completes the link between the physical brain and the nonphysical Mind. (Further ideas related to this link are given in appendix C.) There is one additional thought I will include here, and that is on how the freedom to choose plays out in our daily thoughts.

DETERMINISM & CHOICE IN
THE BRAIN-WAVE FUNCTION

According to quantum mechanics, *each branch* of the brain wave function—with each branch corresponding to a potential thought—is deterministic. Thus, because each potential thought is deterministic, this might lead us to think that our thinking is deterministic. But that is not true because the Mind's attention can move from one determined branch to another.

As an example, suppose you are looking at an orchard. In perceiving the orchard, you might think at first that there is no choice to be made by your Mind, for the wave function of the brain that corresponds to seeing the orchard is deterministic: The light from the orchard deterministically affects your retina, the retina sends deterministic signals to your brain, and the brain deterministically processes those signals.

Even though the branch of the brain wave function corresponding to the response to the orchard signals is deterministic, however, the total wave function is not; it contains many branches besides that one. Thus, there are still many choices. For example, your Mind could choose to put its attention on a branch of the brain wave function that corresponds to listening to the birds in the orchard, rather than on the branch that corresponds to seeing them. Or you could choose to narrow your attention to a particular apple in the orchard. Or you could think about apple pie for dessert.

CHAINS OF THOUGHT

The same reasoning applies to chains of thought. There is a deterministic branch of the wave function corresponding to each chain of thought. Again, though, a particular chain of thought is only one of many branches of the total brain wave function. So there is still choice, because we can choose to keep our attention on the branch of the wave function corresponding to one particular chain, or the Mind can choose another branch to concentrate on.

Most people's Minds tend to make minimal use of that choice, preferring instead to drift with the deterministic flow of the brain. Gaining stronger control of the choice is one of the goals of the mystic.

REVIEW

- The brain wave function has many branches, all existing simultaneously, with each branch corresponding to a neural firing pattern and thus to a potential action or thought.

- The Mind is aware (in a nonordinary sense) of some or all of these branches. It freely chooses which branch—"which thought or action"—to concentrate on and thereby bring into our ordinary, everyday conscious perception.
- Each deterministic chain of thought corresponds to a branch of the brain wave function. We have the freedom to jump out of one chain of thought and into another chain of thought at any moment.

12

PROPERTIES OF THE MIND— PURE INTELLIGENCE

How can I be conscious and you be conscious at the same time and separate?

RUMI

The Mind interpretation of quantum mechanics raises several questions. What are the characteristics of the Mind? Does it have a structure? What is the relation of the Mind to the self? Is each Mind totally isolated from each other Mind?

CHARACTERISTICS OF THE MIND

The most we can infer directly from our interpretation of quantum mechanics is that the nonphysical Mind exists and perceives the wave function. We can, however, infer certain characteristics of the Mind indirectly, based on the assumption that it makes intelligent choices. The Mind presumably has goals; it has emotions that provide the motivation to pursue those goals; it has memory (independent of the brain); and it has the ability to learn, although perhaps not in the "learning facts" sense.

Because the Mind perceives the wave functions of a hundred billion neurons, we can also see that it must be able to deal with complexity. It must have the ability to abstract the essence of all the data it is presented with and to make decisions based on that abstraction. How does the Mind manage all of this? The answer, or at least the beginning of an answer, is that the Mind itself must have a complex structure, a structure that is related to the forms of nonphysical existence.

The nonphysical Mind, at base, is simply archetypal awareness plus intelligence. To function in existence, however, the Mind must make use of some type of nonphysical material or form. The forms are the djinn thought-forms mentioned in chapter 4. These djinn thought-forms are the precursors of physical-brain-based thoughts.

THE MIND & THE SELF

Your self when you exist here on earth consists of your body; your brain, including its neurochemistry and memories; and your Mind, plus a djinn part, as discussed earlier, and an angelic part. (Each human being consists of three parts—physical, djinn, and angelic—plus a Mind. The angelic part is the part that can perceive and act on the angelic plane, and also experience the emotions of that plane.)

Your Mind is the most essential part of your self. It is more you, says Rumi, than things that have happened to you, closer to you than the large artery in your neck. It is the part that will survive death. While we live, the primary tools of the Mind are the body and brain. They give us concrete means of responding to the longings and aspirations of the Mind.

PURE INTELLIGENCE

We consider now the connection between Minds. One of the insights of the mystics is that there is a unity to existence. I will introduce unity into our metaphysical cosmology (this chapter is primarily about metaphysics rather than physics) by assuming there is a single overarching Mind, which is identical to the Pure Intelligence of chapter 3.[1] Pure Intelligence is the highest and most rarified form of intelligence and awareness.

All forms of intelligence and awareness spring from Pure Intelligence. Each individual Mind, in this cosmology is a fragment or aspect of Pure Intelligence. Or to say it another way, the individual Mind is that aspect of Pure Intelligence that is focused on the wave function of a particular individual brain. And each individual Mind, even though it is a part of Pure Intelligence, is assumed to have free, autonomous choice of which branch of the wave function of its associated brain to perceive, and therefore which thought or action to bring into conscious existence.

PURE INTELLIGENCE &
THE CONNECTIONS BETWEEN MINDS

On the physical plane, we appear to be isolated, disconnected individuals. In the Mind cosmology presented here, though, we are all tied together because each of us is an aspect of Pure Intelligence.

One of the goals of the mystic is to scale the heights of awareness and intelligence, and to finally make his or her awareness and intelligence as close to that of Pure Intelligence as possible. That goal can be achieved only after a long journey. As we make the journey toward the Pure Intelligence from which we all spring, however, the isolation between individuals begins to disappear. This makes the effort to become a mystic worthwhile.

•   •   •

This ends our first pass at understanding the nature of the nonphysical aspect of existence and its relation to the physical world. The effort will be taken up again in part 4, from the point of view of the mystic, after we have looked at how the brain functions.

REVIEW

- The Mind, which makes the choice of which quantum branch to perceive, has goals, aspirations, memory, the ability to learn, and the ability to abstract essence. The Mind must therefore have a complex structure.
- The forms the Mind works with are nonphysical djinn thought-forms.
- The Mind is the most essential part of the self.
- Each individual Mind is an aspect of a single overarching Pure Intelligence.
- Pure Intelligence is the source of all intelligence and awareness.
- Each individual Mind has its own autonomous choice of which branch of the individual brain wave function to perceive.
- We are all connected because each of us is an aspect of Pure Intelligence. Thus, the isolation between beings lessens as our perspective approaches that of Pure Intelligence.

13

SUMMARY OF PHYSICS

The basic objective of the physics section is to show that if we assume quantum mechanics is a correct and complete description of the physical universe, then it follows that each of us has a nonphysical Mind that can freely choose our thoughts and actions.

THE MAIN POINTS

FROM CLASSICAL PHYSICS TO QUANTUM MECHANICS

From 1700 until 1900 and after, physicists used classical Newtonian physics to describe successfully many of the phenomena of the physical world. This was a deterministic theory in which the future was mathematically fixed; no free choice, no spontaneity. Then in the early 1900s, experiments were done whose results could not be explained by classical physics. The search for an explanation led, in 1926, to the discovery of quantum mechanics.

Over the past seventy-five years, quantum mechanics has been successfully applied to many, many problems. Its success, internal consistency, and unity argue in favor of its being the final theory of the physical universe, never to be superseded.

THE WAVE FUNCTION

Quantum mechanics is a mathematical theory in which there is an equation, the Schrödinger equation, for the wave function. The equation dictates how the wave function changes in time. The wave function can be visualized as matter spread out in a mist.

MANY POSSIBLE FUTURES: BRANCHES

The wave function typically breaks up into many different parts or branches, with each branch corresponding to a possible future of the physical universe. Thus, the mathematics of quantum mechanics allows many possible futures.

THE NEED FOR AN INTERPRETATION OF QUANTUM MECHANICS

Mathematically, all these futures exist simultaneously in the wave function. But we do not see a blurring together or superposition of them; instead, we perceive events corresponding to only one branch. It is not known why we are consciously aware of only one branch. To explain why, various interpretations of quantum mechanics—conceptual schemes that bridge the gap between the mathematics and our perceptions—have been proposed.

THE PARTICLE INTERPRETATION

To physicists, the most obvious interpretation is to assume there are objectively existing particles. If this is correct, then existence is material-only and there is no mysticism. It cannot be shown to be correct, however, for when the evidence is examined closely, it is found that there is no convincing evidence for the existence of particles. Thus, physics does *not* rule out mysticism.

INTERPRETATION IN WHICH ONLY THE WAVE FUNCTION EXISTS

There are no particles in the mathematics of quantum mechanics; there is only the wave function. In addition, all the particlelike properties—mass, energy, momentum, spin, and charge—can be shown to be properties of the wave function alone. Thus, the evidence favors the existence of the wave function alone, rather than the wave function plus particles (or particles alone). We are therefore free to assume, without contradicting experience, experiment, or theory, that only the wave function exists. The later chapters of the physics part of the book explain the consequences of the idea that only the wave function exists.

NO OBJECTIVE REALITY

We assume that all the branches of the wave function, all the possible futures, continue to coexist forever. Thus, there is no unique objective reality. There are many possible realities, but we perceive only one.

THE MIND PERCEIVES

Why do we perceive only one possible reality or course of events when many coexist in the wave function? To explain why, we must assume each of us has his or her own individual nonphysical Mind. It is the Mind "looking in" from outside physical reality that perceives the wave function. But your Mind perceives only the wave function of your brain, not the wave function of the outer world.

THE MIND FREELY CHOOSES

The wave function of the brain is very complex; it contains a branch corresponding to every one of our possible future thoughts and actions. One example would be a branch corresponding to whistling; another might be tapping the fingers; another, imagining a mountain stream. In a way that is different from our ordinary awareness, the Mind perceives, or is aware of, all these possibilities at once.

Then, from all these coexisting branches, all these potential futures, the Mind can freely choose which branch to *concentrate on* and thereby bring into our usual consciousness. The chosen branch—which might be whistling, for example—thereby effectively changes from potential to actual event. It is the outer result another person would see of your Mind's inner choice.

ATTRIBUTES OF THE MIND

We infer from the Mind's ability to make choices that it has intelligence, goals, and a memory. Further, because the nonphysical Mind must deal with the extreme complexity of the brain's wave function, the Mind itself must have a complex (nonphysical) structure.

PURE INTELLIGENCE

To make our conceptual scheme agree with the unity that the mystic experiences, we assume there is a single overarching Pure Intelligence. Each individual Mind is a fragment or aspect of Pure Intelligence. We each derive our awareness and intelligence from this connection to Pure Intelligence. Each individual Mind is that aspect of Pure Intelligence that focuses its awareness on a particular brain. Each Mind has free, autonomous choice of which potential action or thought to focus on and bring into ordinary consciousness as the effective objective reality.

QUANTUM MECHANICS & MYSTICISM

We have supposed that quantum mechanics, with all its many branches and no particles, is an essentially correct and complete theory of the physical universe. Under that assumption, the Mind interpretation presented here is the only possible interpretation.

From the mystical point of view, the Mind interpretation tells us that each of us is, at base, a nonphysical Mind that makes choices on the wave function of the physical brain. It is an interpretation that is fully consistent with, and even clarifies and elaborates upon, the mystic's position that there is a nonphysical component to existence. The Mind interpretation of quantum mechanics is the bridge between the physical universe and nonphysical existence.

Examples of physical and nonphysical:

Physical. The wave function; all of our usual outer world; ordinary thinking and emotion (that part associated with brain processes).

Nonphysical. The Mind; choice; what is behind brain-based thoughts; higher emotions; life after death.

PART 3

THE BRAIN

INTRODUCTION TO THE BRAIN

*When you realize the difference between the tool and the user,
you will have knowledge.*[1]

IDRIES SHAH

The nature of our existence as human beings is strongly determined by our brain, for every ordinary perception, bodily action, memory, thought, and emotion depends on its functions. If we are to fully understand ourselves, even in a secular sense, it is essential that we have some knowledge of how the brain works.

But there are reasons more directly related to the needs of the aspiring mystic. The mystics of the past had knowledge of what the brain does (although they didn't have as accurate, detailed, and useful a picture as we have now), and how it both enables and limits us. Based on their knowledge of how the brain limits the Mind's freedom, they devised practices to help the aspiring mystic reclaim that freedom. By learning about the brain, you will, like the mystics, be able to see what limitations the brain imposes and how mystical practices can help you surmount those limitations. I will give more details about the link between brain functions and mystical practices in chapter 28, after I have described the practices.

The second reason for the aspiring mystic to study the brain has to do with the separation of reality into this world and the "other" world. We exist on two levels—the physical level of the body, and the nonphysical level of the Mind—and one of the goals of the aspiring mystic is to distinguish between them. That is not so easy because the physical brain-based processes associated with thinking and emotion are intimately interconnected with the workings of the nonphysical Mind.

We can distinguish more readily and accurately between the physical and nonphysical if we are aware of what the brain does and how it does it. Knowledge of the tool—the brain—helps us realize the difference between the tool and the user—the Mind. It helps us distinguish between the part of our experience determined by the characteristics and limitations of the tool and the part more directly created by the Mind. And it thereby helps us distinguish between that part of the self which will survive death and that part which will not.

To understand the mechanisms of perception, thought, and emotion, we need to know a few basic facts about the brain. The basic functional units are its one hundred billion neurons, all of which operate in the same way; when they are stimulated, an electrochemical voltage pulse travels down these long cells. All ordinary thoughts, all sensory perceptions, all ordinary emotions and feelings, and all signals sent to the muscles consist solely of these pulses moving along neurons.

There are several remarkable observations about the relation between these pulses and our experiencing and making sense of the world. First, each pulse, by itself, carries no information—about size, for example, or shape, color, distance, or emotional content; all that information is contained in the organization of the pulses.

Second, when I am looking out my office window at a white pine and the children's swing beyond, the retina of my eye sends millions of pulses per second to my brain. These pulses provide the only information I have about the view from my window. I do not see the trees and swing "directly," for if the visual processing area of the brain is damaged, I literally could not see these objects, even if my eyes were working perfectly. The tree and swing are perceived only through the intermediary mechanism of the neural pulses.

Third, the pattern of the pulses is abstract, with abstract meaning not patternless but patterned at a deeper level; there is nothing in the pattern corresponding *directly* to the color green, for example, or to distance or to the name "white pine" or to the identification of the set of bars and chains as a children's swing.

Finally, the same observations hold true for thinking; abstract patterns of pulses represent concepts as well as objects. Emotions and feelings (at least on the physical level) also correspond solely to patterns of pulses. The net result is that the only way for our brain and Mind to make sense of the outer world of objects and the inner world of thoughts and emotions is to decode an abstract pattern of electrochemical neural pulses.

We do not just perceive, however; we also control. We control our attention—what we see, what we hear, what we think—we control our bodies, and to some extent, we control our emotions. This control has two levels; there are the deterministic control mechanisms built into the brain, and there is the freedom-of-choice control that the nonphysical Mind has over the physical brain.

In the next few chapters, we will look at how the brain makes sense of the world and at how both the brain and the Mind exert control over our thoughts and actions.

THE SYNAPSE

The brain has two ways of organizing the flow of neural pulses. The first uses synapses, the gaps between neurons, and the second uses large-scale groupings of neurons that specialize in certain tasks. I will describe synaptic mechanism here and large-scale organization in chapter 16.

The synapse, the junction between two neurons, controls whether a pulse in one neuron is passed onto another neuron. Understanding the operation of the synapse is crucial for understanding memory, the associative process, emotions, and moods. Even more important, the synapses are critical in controlling the flow of thoughts, for it is through the mechanisms of the synapse that the Mind can freely choose which thoughts we think and which actions we take.

THE FUNCTIONING OF THE NEURON

Before we can understand how the synapse works, we must understand the basics of the neuron. Figure 15.1 is a diagram of a typical neuron in the brain:

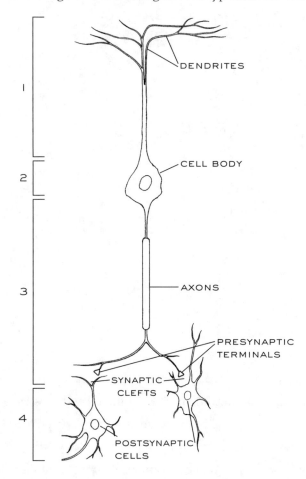

FIGURE 15.1 *Diagram of a typical brain neuron. The numbers on the left refer to stages in its operation.*

Biologically, it is a single cell, even though it can be very long—up to a meter long in the spinal column. Each neuron consists of many dendrites at the top, a cell body in the middle, and a long axon that breaks into many branches at its end. A branch of the axon from one neuron nearly touches another neuron's dendrites at a synapse, or junction between cells. Each of the brain's hundred billion neurons has an average of five synaptic connections with each of a thousand other neurons, for a total of five thousand connections per neuron. So the brain is very complex indeed.

Each neuron functions in essentially the same way; when suitably stimulated, it sends an electrochemical pulse down along its length. There are four stages in the process:

1. The dendrites are stimulated by neurotransmitter chemicals from other neurons. This causes a *dendritic* voltage pulse to move down the dendrite to the cell body.

2. The cell body simultaneously receives voltage pulses from many of its hundreds of dendrites. These voltage pulses are electrochemically combined in the cell body. There are both excitatory synapses that send positive pulses and inhibitory synapses that send negative pulses, with at least half the synapses being inhibitory. The inhibitory pulses give stability to brain processes, preventing epilepsylike, out-of-control cascades of excitatory pulses.

3. If the net sum of the incoming dendritic pulses—excitatory minus inhibitory—is large enough, that is, if the neuron has received positive synaptic stimuli from enough other neurons, a pulse is sent down the axon. This axonic pulse is an all-or-nothing response to the sum of the incoming signals. Either it is sent or it is not; a partial pulse is never sent. The pulse always starts at the cell body and moves down the axon. The neuron is said to fire when it sends a pulse down the axon. As stated previously, the axonic pulse is the basic mechanism of the brain. All our thoughts and perceptions[1] consist simply of sequences of these pulses.

4. The fourth stage of the cell's operation is the transmission of the axonic pulse to the dendrites of another (postsynaptic) cell at the synapse.

THE SYNAPSE

The synapse is the junction between neurons, the place where a neural pulse passes from one neuron to the next. A pulse in the presynaptic branch does not always produce a pulse in the postsynaptic dendrite. Control of pulse-propagating conditions at the synapse is critical in controlling the sequence of pulses, and thus the flow of thoughts, in the brain. Because of this pivotal role, we must understand the synapse to understand memory, emotions, control of attention, and the way in which control of the flow of thoughts is related to quantum mechanics and freedom of choice.

OPERATION OF A SYNAPSE

A synapse has three parts as is shown in figure 15.2: a presynaptic terminal, a synaptic cleft, and a postsynaptic membrane, which is part of the next neuron.

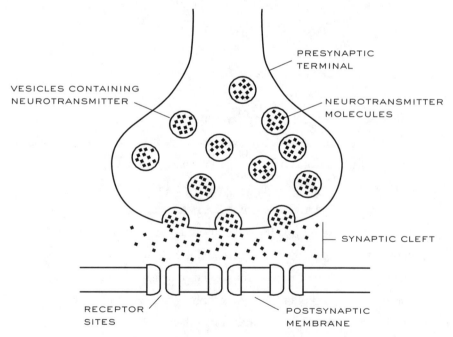

FIGURE 15.2 *Diagram of a synapse.*

All these parts are minute, with typical dimensions being considerably less than a thousand atoms (one ten-thousandth of a millimeter). Here is how a synapse works: A neural pulse in a presynaptic neuron triggers a discharge of neurotransmitter molecules into the synaptic cleft.

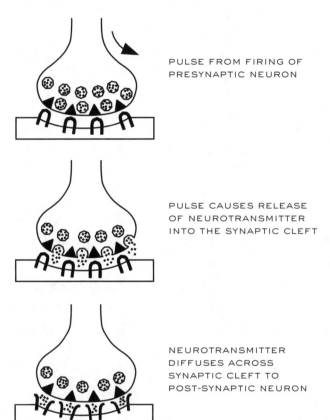

PULSE FROM FIRING OF PRESYNAPTIC NEURON

PULSE CAUSES RELEASE OF NEUROTRANSMITTER INTO THE SYNAPTIC CLEFT

NEUROTRANSMITTER DIFFUSES ACROSS SYNAPTIC CLEFT TO POST-SYNAPTIC NEURON

FIGURE 15.3 *Operation of a synapse.*

The molecules quickly diffuse across the synaptic cleft to the postsynaptic membrane. Receptors for the neurotransmitters are embedded in the post-synaptic membrane. The receptors work on a lock-and-key principle; each receptor, or lock, is receptive to a certain neurotransmitter molecule, or key.

When the appropriate neurotransmitter molecule attaches itself to the receptor, a postsynaptic dendritic pulse is initiated (stage 1 in the neuron's function). This pulse then travels down the dendrite to the neural body, where it is summed with the other dendritic pulses (stage 2 in the neuron's function).

SYNAPTIC EFFICIENCY & NEUROCHEMICALS

EFFICIENCY

A presynaptic pulse doesn't always induce a postsynaptic pulse; on average, it does so only half the time. This average varies widely at different synapses, however, due to neurochemical details.

NEUROCHEMISTRY

There are at least fifty different neurotransmitter molecules that migrate across the synaptic cleft, with a specialized receptor for each one on the postsynaptic terminal (but only two or three neurotransmitters are used in a particular synapse, not all fifty). This large number of different neurotransmitters allows for more diversity and subtlety in our thoughts and emotions. There are also neurochemicals other than neurotransmitters whose role is to modulate the effect of the neurotransmitters.

EXCITATORY & INHIBITORY NEUROTRANSMITTERS

As mentioned earlier, there can be both positive and negative pulses in a neuron's dendrites. Neurotransmitters that trigger positive pulses are called excitatory, and those that trigger negative pulses are called inhibitory.

CAFFEINE & THE SELF

To give an idea of the complex action of neurochemicals, I will explain how caffeine acts as a stimulant. Glutamate is the primary excitatory neurotransmitter, so if there is more glutamate, there will be more positive, excitatory pulses, and this increases alertness. To balance this natural stimulant, the body produces adenosine, a neurochemical that inhibits the release of glutamate. When adenosine acts on the presynaptic terminal, less glutamate is produced, and alertness decreases.

The role of caffeine is to block the effects of adenosine, so drinking coffee inhibits adenosine's ability to inhibit glutamate. This causes more glutamate to be released, which stimulates your nervous system, so you feel more alert, even jittery.

This example stimulates a couple of thoughts on the self. First, it is not really "you" that changes when you drink coffee; it is only your neurochemistry. The counter observation is that your Mind's view of itself is influenced by events that happen frequently to its associated body. So drinking coffee can, over time, change the Mind's view of itself, and this amounts to a change in your self after all.

EMOTIONS

There are regions in the central part of the brain whose functions are concerned with emotions. When neurons in these regions are triggered, particularly by strong emotions, specific neurochemicals are produced throughout the brain. These selectively alter the efficiency of various sets of synapses, thereby coloring our thoughts. When you are angry, for example, the emotion-related part of your brain triggers the release of neurochemicals that affect your range of thoughts.

Our moods are also correlated with neurochemistry. Neuroscientist Antonio Damasio, who studies the relation between emotional states and neurochemistry, gives two examples of this.[2] In the first, elation, there is suppression of the inhibitory neurotransmitters, with the suppression coming from the brain's release of neurochemicals. The typical reaction to this is that you have many more thoughts than usual, with a wider range of topics, but you don't dwell as long on each idea. The extreme of this is the manic state. In contrast, in sadness, there is suppression of the excitatory neurotransmitters. Here, you generate fewer thoughts and the range of topics is narrow. You are slower in your movements and have less appetite and interest in novel ideas. Sadness carried to extreme is depression.

QUANTUM MECHANICS, THE SYNAPSES & CHOICE OF THOUGHTS

We switch now from neurochemistry to the quantum mechanics of the synapse. Because the synapse is so small—the synaptic cleft is only thirty-five atoms wide—quantum mechanics is relevant there. The way in which quantum mechanics enters is that the wave function of the synapse will have two quantum branches, a branch in which a presynaptic pulse triggers a postsynaptic pulse and a branch in which it does not trigger a postsynaptic pulse.

It is here that the Mind interpretation comes in. Because this branching is internal to the brain, the Mind can choose which branch to concentrate on (and it is that branch that becomes physical reality). Thus, by concentrating on the "pulse" branch (so that a pulse "actually" occurs), the Mind can effectively change the efficiency of the synapse from 50 percent to 100 percent; or by concentrating on the "no pulse" branch (so there is, in effect, no pulse), it can effectively change the efficiency from 50 percent to zero. (Remember that, on average, a pulse is triggered half the time.) In our everyday life, the Mind does this concentrating—which is beneath the level of our ordinary consciousness—on one branch or another very easily and naturally; it is not something we have to put conscious effort into.

Finally, the synapses are the sole mechanism by which the flow of thoughts is controlled. Thus, by choosing which branch to concentrate on—the one triggering a postsynaptic pulse or the one not triggering a pulse—and by doing this simultaneously at many synapses, the Mind can effectively choose which neurons fire and therefore which thoughts we think.

THE COMPUTERLIKE ASPECTS OF THE BRAIN—VISION & MEMORY

In the last chapter, I outlined the functioning of the microscopic synapse, which is a critical part of our makeup because it is the physical mechanism through which the nonphysical Mind controls our thoughts. In this chapter, I will discuss the large-scale organizational aspects of the brain. To illustrate how this computerlike operation enables us to make sense of the world, I will explain how the brain recognizes what we see.

Why is this important to the mystic? Because it is critical to understand what in our experience is due to the operation of our physical body as opposed to our nonphysical Mind. Understanding how the brain recognizes what we see also emphasizes the complex, abstract decoding process constantly going on behind our seemingly effortless perception of the concrete world of people and houses and cars.

SPECIALIZED AREAS OF THE BRAIN—VISION

The brain has an outer surface, the cerebral cortex, that is involved in perception and thinking. The cortex is neatly divided into two nearly identical right and left halves by a deep fissure down the middle. Each half is divided into about fifty areas, with each area carrying out a specialized task. The outer layer of the left side is shown in figure 16.1, with the conventional numbering for the areas.

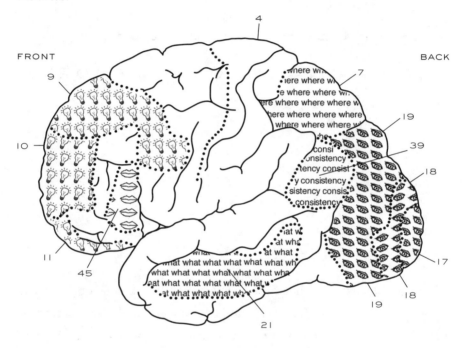

FIGURE 16.1 *Functional areas of the brain. Each side of the brain is divided into about fifty different areas, each of which has its own specific function. A few of the areas of the left side, with the conventional numbering, are shown. The lightbulb (for ideas) indicates the thinking part, the eye the seeing part, and the mouth, speech.*

To illustrate how the brain makes sense of what we see, I will analyze the processes that go on when you look at the cross in figure 16.2.

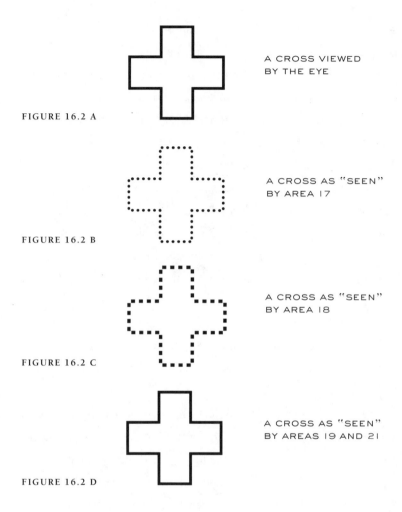

FIGURE 16.2 A

A CROSS VIEWED
BY THE EYE

FIGURE 16.2 B

A CROSS AS "SEEN"
BY AREA 17

FIGURE 16.2 C

A CROSS AS "SEEN"
BY AREA 18

FIGURE 16.2 D

A CROSS AS "SEEN"
BY AREAS 19 AND 21

Light from the cross enters the eye and is converted into patterns of neural pulses by the specialized neurons of the retina at the back of the eye. The neural pulses are sent via the million neurons in the optic nerve to area 17 at the back of the brain where the first analysis of the visual data is performed. There, because of the cleverly arranged interconnections between optic nerve neurons and area 17 neurons, the area 17 neurons are able to "find" small sections of the edges in the figure of the cross, shown as short dashes in Figure 16.2b.

This data is then sent to area 18 where the small sections are put together into longer segments, as in figure 16.2c. Again the data is sent forward, this time to area 19, which puts the line segments together and assembles a more or less complete picture of the cross, figure 16.2d. But it is not an actual picture of the cross (even though we have drawn it that way, and the geometry of the cross is retained somewhat in the pattern of the firing neurons); instead it is a neuronal encoding of the shape of the cross.

This encoded message from area 19 is sent to area 7 (denoted by *where* in figure 16.1), which is able to deduce from the visual contextual clues (also encoded as neural pulses) just where the cross is located (about twenty inches in front of your eyes). The encoded message from area 19 is also sent to area 21 (denoted by *what* in figure 16.1), where it is compared to a memory bank of other encoded messages gleaned from experience. And, lo and behold, it finds a match with the encoded message for "cross," no matter what the size and location of the cross. Finally, areas 21 and 7 send their neurally encoded findings on "what" and "where" to area 39, which checks for consistency (see figure 16.1).

If we want to say the name of the object, the area 39 results are sent to area 45, which holds the rules of grammar, vocabulary, and the sound structure of words. (Stroke victims with damage to this area cannot put words together into grammatically proper phrases and sentences.) The sound structure of "cross" is sent to a special premotor part of area 9, where the connection between sounds and the movements of the tongue, mouth, vocal cords, and so on is first made. This information is then sent to the motor area, area 4, which further organizes it, and then sends the appropriate neural signals to the muscles of the lips, tongue, and jaw for the actual speaking of the word *cross*.

To summarize, the brain uses an abstract binary code ("no pulse" or "pulse") to encode what we see. The decoding consists of a neural analysis of the pulse pattern, which is then compared to a memory bank of neural patterns so we recognize what we see. It is interesting that thinking—What should I cook for dinner?—is carried out by the same neural encoding method, with certain patterns of pulses corresponding to certain concepts (such as "I," "cook," "dinner"). Thus, the only thing that is of significance in the brain—the only thing that the Mind recognizes—is the abstract pattern of neural pulses.

MEMORY

Memory is a major factor in our experience of the physical world. It weaves the events of our lives into a coherent tapestry. It is an essential survival tool, allowing us to learn from experience. And, in addition to being involved in conscious recollection, it is also essential for many of the functions of the brain, including emotions, body movements, perception, the associative process, and imagination. I will describe here the basics of memory and the consequences of the memory process for the aspiring mystic, including the way in which it can limit our perception of existence.

The neural basis of memory is a circuit of neurons with efficient synapses— 95 percent efficient, say, rather than the 50 percent average—that enable the neural pulses to flow easily from one neuron to the next. It is, in effect, a circuit engraved within the tangle of neurons. Because there is this single explanation of memory, it was once thought that there was a single type of memory. That is now known to be incorrect, though; there are several types of memory.

In what we normally think of as memory—declarative memory, retention of facts and events—it usually takes a number of repetitions to establish the memory; we need to repeat a list of names several times before it becomes part of our permanent memory (that is, before the circuit becomes permanently engraved). Once set, however, the memory can last for years.

Strong emotional memories can also last for years, in fact, there is evidence that they last a good deal longer than declarative memory. In addition, these memories are often formed by just one repetition. The neuroscientist, Joseph LeDoux, gives a striking example of the separation of conscious declarative memory and emotional memory, and the fact that emotional memory is not always subject to conscious recall:

> In the early part of this century, a French physician named Edouard Claparede examined a female patient who, as a result of brain damage, had seemingly lost all ability to create new memories. Each time Claparede walked into the room he had to reintroduce himself to her, as she had no recollection of having seen him before. The memory problem was so severe that if Claparede left the room and returned a few minutes later, she wouldn't remember having seen him.
>
> One day, he tried something new. He entered the room, and, as on every other day, he held out his hand to greet her. In typical fashion she shook his hand. But when their hands met, she quickly pulled hers back, for Claparede had concealed a tack in his palm and had pricked her with it. The next time he returned to the room to greet her, she still had no recognition of him, but she refused to shake his hand. She could not tell him why she would not shake hands with him, but she wouldn't do it.[1]

Each of us, I think, has not-clearly-remembered emotional memories that influence our behavior.

Working memory is short-term memory, existing for less than a couple of minutes, located in the prefrontal region (areas 9, 10, and 11 in figure 16.1). The contents of working memory are the facts and concepts the brain is currently paying attention to and manipulating. (Should I go to the potluck supper tonight? How do I construct this sentence?) This content is what we are consciously aware of.

Bodily memory is the memory of all the bodily skills we have learned—walking, writing, the skills of an athlete or a musician. They are stored partly in the premotor and motor areas, including area 4, and partly in the cerebellum, a region of the brain near the top of the brain stem.

There are also other types of memory: procedural—memory of rules such as those for playing chess; memory of language; and memory of music (which often outlasts other memories in Alzheimer's patients).

MEMORY CATEGORIES

Memories are organized into categories, presumably as a more efficient way of filing them for potential use. Research on patients with localized brain damage (usually to area 21) has revealed that the categories are many and varied: small tools, animals, musical instruments, faces, fruits, vegetables, body parts, facial expressions, and so on. Sometimes they are modality-specific; one patient could recognize musical instruments by sound but not by sight.

One of the interesting and important characteristics of memory circuits and their organization into categories is that the memory structure is specific to each person. With a few possible exceptions, such as the general face category, there are no category memory circuits in our brain at birth; instead, they are determined by our individual experience. These categories are a large part of the conventional definition of "you," and they help to form the frame of reference from which you view the world. (Choose your memories carefully!)

MEMORY CATEGORIES & LIMITATION

Memory is an indispensable part of our neural apparatus, but because its influence is so dominant, it can limit our thinking and perception. All our perceptions are compared to memory—Is that a bird? A plane?—and after a certain age, the brain greatly prefers a match to a memory rather than a novel, nonmatchable input. The preference is so great, in fact, that *data is often forced into pre-existing categories*. This happens occasionally in factual situations, but the influence of memory categories becomes more important as you move toward more complex and ambiguous situations.

Suppose, for example, that two people meet a stranger. One might have well-developed categories in the area of clothes and body language, while the other might be more attuned to the nuances of the voice. Thus, because of the selective perception induced by their different categories, they could come away with very different impressions of the stranger.

INTUITION

Your Mind has access to knowledge that does not come from physical perception or the workings of your brain. When this intuitive knowledge is forced to conform to the memory categories of your brain, it loses much of its truth and creative power. The mystic learns ways to avoid this loss.

IMAGINATION

One of the most interesting properties of the human brain is its ability to imagine.[2] For the purpose of explanation, we can divide imagination into two steps: calling up an image, and then manipulating that image. The manipulation is done in working memory according to certain neurally prescribed rules. Unfortunately, this most interesting process, which is intimately related to problem-solving and creativity, is not well understood.

Calling up an image involves the visual system. To see how visual imagination works, imagine a blue bowl on a picnic table ten feet away. First, your prefrontal cortex (areas 9, 10, and 11) sends a neural message back down the visual chain (area 39 to 21 and 7 to 19 to 18). The message activates certain memory categories corresponding to blue bowl, table, ten feet, bowl on table, much as if you were actually looking at a bowl on the table.

Thus, the parts of the brain that would be activated in perceiving a real bowl on a real picnic table are activated in the imaginary case also. The brain can nearly always tell the difference between an image induced by an actual bowl and an imagined one, however, because of the relative weakness of the "perception" signal and the lack of feedback from the eyes in the case of the imagined bowl.

DREAMING

Visual imagination is an activation of the visual apparatus by internal processes, rather than by what the eye sees. Dreaming makes use of the same neural processes as visual imagination, but the conscious checks and controls we have when awake are turned off, so the dreams take on a fantastic quality.

CONCEPTS

The same sort of activation from memory occurs when solving problems. In this case, however, in addition to visual images, we also bring up concepts from memory, and then manipulate them (with concepts being stored as engraved neural circuits, just as visual memories are).

17

EMOTIONS—CONTROL OF ATTENTION

We might ask "What is truly 'me'?" Many people would say their emotions—their nonreasoned evaluations such as delight, sorrow, joy, fear—are the core of "me." And so it might be surprising to learn that—just as with perception, memory, and thinking—there are also neural processes in the brain corresponding to emotions. Awareness of these deterministic neural processes is useful on the mystical path for several reasons.

First, aspiring mystics need to be aware of these processes so they don't get unduly caught up in the automatic responses generated by strong brain-based emotions. Second, there are weaker brain-based emotions that constantly, and mostly subconsciously, determine our choice of thoughts and thereby deprive us of our freedom of thought. The aspiring mystic needs to become aware of these low-level, thought-guiding emotions and learn ways to regain the freedom of thought and intuitive insight that they rob us of. Finally, there are deeper, non-brain-based emotions that are a more accurate guide to our intelligence and actions. We will still experience emotions after our physical bodies die, and these are the nonphysical emotions. We can, and do to some extent, experience those emotions here also. Non-brain-based emotions, such as love, friendship, and joy at creativity, may still have a neural (i.e., bodily) correlate, but they are not *based* in the brain. It is most useful to be able to distinguish between the physically based emotions and the deeper, nonphysical ones. The material in this section is a starting point, but there are also practices you must do to become fully aware of the deeper emotions.

EMOTIONAL APPARATUS OF THE BRAIN

The emotional processes of the brain are not as well understood as perceptual processes. Nevertheless, the general outline of the neural processes related to emotions is fairly well understood. The pivotal structure is the amygdala, a part of the limbic system in the center of the brain. The amygdala receives neural input from a number of areas—our eyes, our ears, our thoughts—makes an evaluation of the emotional content of the input (based in part on comparison to our emotional memories), and then transmits the results of that evaluation to other areas—perhaps to our prefrontal thinking cortex or the adrenal glands. Because these processes are somewhat involved, I will not give them in detail.

EMOTIONS & DECISION-MAKING

We may think of emotions as having to do only with the way we feel, but it turns out that these evaluative reactions are of great importance in our everyday decision-making. Damasio made this point by describing patients who had damage to the neural emotional apparatus, but not to the rest of the brain. He found they had trouble making even the simplest decisions; they could not decide, for example, whether to go for a walk or make a phone call. And the moral component of their decision-making was impaired. Their inability to make normal decisions was not due to damage to their logical apparatus, for that was normal. Instead, they were unable to put an evaluative tag, such as interesting or repulsive, on the various options, and it turns out that these nonlogical evaluations are critical in making decisions.

MICROEMOTIONS

Not only are emotional evaluative reactions necessary for making obvious decisions, they are also subtly at work in making evaluative decisions millisecond by millisecond. To our conscious minds, it appears that one thought logically follows another. But our brains are continually receiving a superabundance of data, both from our external senses and our internal thoughts. And if you pay close attention to your thought processes, you can see that the superabundance of data causes many thoughts to arise almost simultaneously. These multiple prethoughts are put through a subconscious emotional evaluation, a weeding-out process, and only one makes it to consciousness. This constant, millisecond-by-millisecond evaluative process, mediated by microemotions, is a major determinant of how and what we think. It is important to be aware of this process and to find ways to counter the biases inevitably associated with it. It is also important to be aware of the mindset from which these microemotions arise, as I will discuss later.

FEELINGS

Even though both emotion and perception involve neural processes in the brain, emotions *feel* different from perceptions. There are, I believe, three reasons for this. One was formulated by William James, who proposed that there is a bodily reaction—for example, quickened heartbeat, shallow breathing—associated with emotion, but not with perception, and it is, according to

James, the perception of the bodily reaction that constitutes the difference between emotion and perception. I do not believe these bodily and neurochemical reactions fully account for the feel of emotions, however.

The second reason for the feel of emotions has been given by Joseph LeDoux. Perception is based on one set of neural processes—those in areas 17, 18, 19, 41, 42, and so on—while emotion is based on another set of neural processes—those in the amygdala, the hypothalamus, and other central parts of the brain. This leads to the suggestion that part of the difference in feeling between perception and emotion comes about because the "conscious awareness center"—probably the prefrontal cortex—is receiving input from different types of brain processes. That is, *perception* is the word we use for conscious awareness of the perceptual (visual, auditory, somatosensory) brain processes, while *feeling* is the word we use for conscious awareness of emotional brain processes.

There is also a third reason for the difference in feel between perception and emotion: Many emotions have their roots in the nonphysical planes, and this adds its own feel. The problem, from a mystic's point of view, is that we give undue attention to the physical component of emotion and forget that the truer emotions are those experienced by the Mind in the djinn and angelic planes, which we will come to later.

ATTENTION

One of our most important human qualities is that we can be consciously aware. We are not aware of everything at once, however; we focus our attention. The following examples illustrate our wide range of focus and the ease with which we control our attention:

• Listen for a moment to the sounds around you.

- Feel your tongue in your mouth.
- Focus on the period at the end of this sentence.
- Think of a word that means the opposite of *tall*.
- Lift one foot.
- Imagine a gold pyramid. Run your finger along one edge.
- Watch your thoughts, what your brain is doing.

Because control of the brain's attention is so central, you must understand it if you are to understand the nature of human existence. This understanding is also necessary for the aspiring mystic because mastery of awareness is a hallmark of the accomplished mystic, who can, on a mundane level be aware of several conversations at once. They do not daydream, gossip, express negative thoughts (many seldom think negative thoughts), or dwell on nonessential problems. They are very aware of you when you are around them. They are very aware of the effect their words and actions will have. And they are almost always aware of their connection to the higher aspects of existence (in religious terms, aware of the presence of God).

There are three successively more refined levels of control of attention in the brain: a general level of alertness, ranging from deep sleep to full alertness; a more specific control of attention by the thalamus; and the detailed control of attention by the prefrontal cortex. And beyond the attention of the brain is the awareness of the Mind.

To appreciate what happens in the brain when we put our attention on something, we must start at the neuronal level. Attention is related to which neurons are firing; roughly, our attention is on that collection of neuronal circuits—corresponding to some object or thought—that has the highest level of firing. Thus, to understand attention, we need to understand how the firing of neurons is controlled. The explanation I will give, based on the relative efficiencies of the various synapses, is not the full story, but it gives the general idea.

THE FIRST LEVEL OF CONTROL—THE RETICULAR FORMATION

The general level of alertness is mediated by the reticular (meaning netlike) formation, located in the brain stem, just above the end of the spinal column. The neurons here reach to all parts of the cortex and can send neural messages that control all the synaptic efficiencies. When we are awake, our synapses have an average efficiency of 50 percent. But in deep sleep, the reticular formation sends messages that activate neurochemicals that reduce the average efficiency to, say, 10 percent. Because of this reduction, there are very few neural pulses circulating in the brain in deep sleep, which is equivalent to saying that we have virtually no thoughts we are aware of. Those suppressing neurochemicals are no longer present in the waking state, and so, in that state, with its 50 percent neural efficiency, we have many neural pulses and thus many thoughts.

THE SECOND LEVEL OF CONTROL—THE THALAMUS

The thalamus, located in the central part of the brain, provides a second way of controlling efficiencies. (There is both a left and a right thalamus, but I will refer to them as if there were only one.) The thalamus acts as a gate for virtually all input to the cortex. All neural pulses from the optic nerve are routed through one part, or nucleus, of the thalamus, all auditory data through another nucleus, touch data through another, and emotional data from within the central part of the brain through still another. The neural motor output to the muscles also goes through a nucleus of the thalamus. By adjusting the efficiencies in the various nuclei, the thalamus is able to suppress selectively various neural messages.

As an example, suppose you decide to direct your attention toward listening to a parakeet rather than looking at it. How does your brain do that? The thinking prefrontal cortex sends a neural message to the thalamus telling it to suppress all input (visual, touch) except the auditory. When that is done, the only region of your brain that generates enough neural pulses to reach the conscious level is the auditory part, and so that is what you pay attention to.

The converse of this process is that if you want to shut out the parakeet's singing, your prefrontal cortex tells your thalamus to inhibit auditory input.

There may be some analog of the thalamus on the nonphysical planes. For various reasons, the Mind may have told this nonphysical analog to shut out nonphysical perception. If so we would have poor intuition as a consequence.

DREAMS

In REM (rapid eye movement) or paradoxical sleep, the combination of reticular formation and thalamic control boosts the efficiencies up to near 50 percent for some parts of the prefrontal cortex, but they still strongly suppress sensory input and motor output as in deep sleep. The prefrontal cortex, however, can imagine, associate, and form memories somewhat as usual, but it cannot readily control the flow of thoughts (the "thought-controlling" region must still have low efficiencies).

THE THIRD LEVEL OF CONTROL—THE PREFRONTAL CORTEX

Suppose we return to the seven attention-focusing examples mentioned on pages 140–141. How is the attention focusing carried out? How do you instruct your brain to change its focus from the period at the end of the sentence to imagining a gold pyramid? We know that the prefrontal cortex is involved and that it must make use of processes similar to those used in imagination, but other than that we do not know how the brain carries out this fine-tuned control.

THE MATERIALIST'S VIEW VERSUS THE MYSTIC'S VIEW OF AWARENESS

What neuroscientists understand even less than control of attention is how, or why, the contents of the prefrontal cortex are what we are consciously aware of. A materialist might suggest an answer along the following lines: Suppose you choose a particular letter on this page of print and concentrate on it. Then concentrate on the details of the letter. What is occurring is that the object of your attention is what your brain is currently working on or manipulating or examining—the letter in this case. That is, attention is not static but dynamic, a process.

I think the materialist's answer is correct up to a point; it describes the neural correlate of attention reasonably well. But the mystic would say that, rather than the brain perceiving the brain, it is the Mind that perceives the neural pulse patterns of the brain (and chooses our actions and thoughts).

NONCONSCIOUS CONTROL OF AWARENESS

What determines what we are aware of? Sometimes it is determined by what we perceive. Sometimes it is deliberately chosen by the conscious self. But often, what we are aware of is determined by nonconscious, mechanistic processes in the brain. The two most prominent of these are association and microemotions.

The semantic distinctions among awareness, attention, and consciousness are not entirely clear. In this chapter, I use *awareness* as the most basic term (basically applying to the Mind), while *attention* corresponds to something that happens in the brain. Moreover, there are gradations of attention. In some situations, such as explicitly switching from seeing to hearing, attention and its control seems to be sharply defined. In everyday life situations, however, there is a gradation ranging from more deliberate and conscious attention to less deliberate and conscious. *Conscious* attention corresponds to being aware not only of the object of perception, but also of the *act* of perception—awareness of being aware.

ASSOCIATION

Association is the process whereby one thought or perception reminds us of another, with a string of associations often resulting in a long, not-consciously-directed chain of thoughts. For example, the word *barn* might remind you of hay, then sneezing, then fields of ragweed, then butterflies, and so on. This not-consciously-directed flow of associated thoughts is useful, because it brings to mind many essential, related ideas. Unless you have carefully trained your mind, though, mechanistic association dominates your thought processes and reduces your freedom of thought.

Mystics are wary of mechanistic processes that restrict mental freedom, so they perform various practices to ensure that the associative process does not dominate their mental processes. Further, it is difficult to separate the brain-based associative thoughts that enter our consciousness from Mind-based intuitive knowledge. To be able to separate them, it helps to become aware, by introspection, of the way association works in your own mind. Then you can begin to distinguish thoughts that don't have the same feel as associatively generated thoughts.

NEUROCHEMICALS & ASSOCIATION

Emotion can strongly affect the associative process. First, strong emotions release neurochemicals in the brain that selectively affect the efficiency of different sets of synapses. The associative chains of thought you experience when you are very angry or fearful are quite different from your chains of thoughts under normal circumstances.

The same neurochemical effect can be associated with dreaming. A dream will often leave a neurochemical residue that can affect the content of your thoughts for hours. Moods, which are usually lower level and longer lasting than strong emotions, affect us through the same selective neurochemical mechanism. Because of this, we can consciously alter our moods by participating in activities that alter our neurochemistry—breathing practices, exercise, massage, listening to music, and so on.

RATIONALIZATION

The brain seeks to make sense out of events. It is a machine for making a coherent, unified story out of minimal data, both perceptual data and stream-of-thought data. To do this, it sometimes uses spurious associations or rationalizations. A fascinating illustration of this occurred in an experiment with split-brain epileptic patients, each of whose corpus callosums—a large bundle of nerves that connects the right and left halves of the brain—had been surgically severed to prevent seizures.[1] Normally, the two sides communicate through the corpus callosum so both halves have the same information. In the split-brain patients, however, there was no communication between the left side, which (normally) controls the speech mechanisms, and the right side, which cannot verbally express what it thinks or feels.

In this experiment, different pictures were shown to the two sides of the brain. (This is possible because the right and left side of each retina is connected only to the left, and right side, respectively of the brain.) The right, nonverbal, side was shown a winter scene. From among four choices of pictures—a snow shovel, a chicken, a leaf, and a pen—the left hand, controlled by the right side, pointed to a snow shovel.

The left, verbal, side was shown a picture of a chicken's claw. The right hand, controlled by the left side, chose, from among the same four choices, a picture of a chicken.

VERBAL LEFT BRAIN	NONVERBAL RIGHT BRAIN
Shown chicken claw. *Pointed to chicken.*	*Shown snow scene.* *Pointed to snow shovel.*

This was just as expected, showing that each half of the brain was intelligent. When asked why the nonverbal hand pointed to a snow shovel, however, the split-brained patient—via the verbal side, which *was not* aware of the winter scene sent to the nonverbal side but *was* aware of the "nonverbal" hand pointing to the snow shovel—said, *seriously,* "Oh, that was to shovel out the chicken coop."

"Why the snow shovel?"

VERBAL LEFT BRAIN (UNAWARE OF SNOW SCENE)	NONVERBAL RIGHT BRAIN
To shovel out the chicken coop.	*Can't answer verbally.*

An association was manufactured by the verbal half in this example (there was no chicken coop mentioned in the experiment; it was a complete fabrication by the patient) to preserve the appearance of rationality. The question is, how much of our own daily thinking involves these manufactured, spurious associations, even though the two halves of a normal brain communicate quite well? More than we suspect or wish, I would guess.

There is one other point that this experiment illustrates to the mystic. The information that the nonverbal side had was correct, but because the information did not go through the rational, verbal apparatus, the verbal side did not trust the nonverbal information. In just the same way, we rationalize away—ignore, distort—intuitive information because it does not come through our rational, verbal apparatus.

MICROEMOTIONS

As mentioned before, there is a second way in which chains of thought are mechanistically guided. In just a couple of seconds, the brain presents us with many, many potential directions for the flow of the chain of thoughts. The many decisions about which chain of thought to follow are usually made nonconsciously, based on the nonconsciously perceived "greatest gain."

The perceived greatest gain—which might take the form of simple interest, familiarity, psychological or emotional energy, avoidance of pain or effort, or ego enhancement—is usually *mechanistically* evaluated by a set of neurally encoded preference rules (rather than by our conscious selves) that have been developed over our lifetime. These rules are encoded as microemotions—*micro* both because they are not full-blown emotions and because they operate on a very short time scale. As examples of how microemotions influence your chain of thoughts, be aware of the subtle evaluative processes that channel your thoughts when you daydream or dwell for a long time on problems. This mostly nonconscious selection process goes on almost continuously.

Mystics seek to become aware of nonconscious biases that arise from the mechanistic operation of their brains and learn how to allow for them, how to override them when necessary, and how to get rid of them permanently when appropriate.

MICROEMOTIONS & INTUITION

In addition to the associative process, the emotional preferences of your brain-Mind can—and usually do—interfere with your reception of intuitive knowledge. To lessen the influence of these microemotions that mechanistically guide your thoughts, you need to develop indifference. This means you become less concerned about things going your way and more interested in how things "really are."

MINDSETS

The collection of all your memory categories together with your bank of familiar concepts and preferences forms your mindset, your overall perspective on yourself and the external world. As you grow older, this mindset, the sum total of the memory, conceptual, and behavioral circuits in your brain, often fossilizes into a limiting point of view—a habitual interpretation laid on external events and intuitive insights, and a habitual reaction to them.

As examples of mindsets, you may always see others as a threat; you may feel yourself inadequate to the challenge of events; you may habitually approach life analytically, with wisecracks, or tiredness, or excessive optimism or pessimism. These mindsets arise because you (your Mind) have assigned more and more authority to the nonconscious associative process and guiding microemotions, with their dependence on habitual categories—factual, behavioral, conceptual—and have abandoned the conscious, fresh appreciation of existence; you are not living in the present moment.

LIMITATIONS

This fossilization of the categories of the brain is closely associated with a severe narrowing of the range of your nonphysical Mind's awareness. That is, in addition to developing a limiting brain-based mindset, you also develop a limiting mindset, a mindset that stays with you after you die. The mystic abhors limiting mindsets and performs practices designed to uproot them.

PART 4

METAPHYSICS

18

THE ANGELIC PLANE—EMOTION

Mystics are experts on the nonphysical worlds. They did not acquire their expertise simply by reading books; they became experts by learning to experience those worlds. Nevertheless, there are advantages to having a conceptual knowledge of the other worlds such as that given in this book: It helps you to remove conceptual blocks to mysticism by making it rationally palatable; it helps you to begin to experience the other planes; it gives you a better understanding of your personality and inclinations; it puts your existence here on earth in a context that allows you to better order your life; and it is a motivating description of the prize you are after. My goal in the next few chapters is to describe the nature of nonphysical existence in a way that will give you the motivation and conceptual basis for learning to experience those worlds.

•   •   •

The lowest level of existence as mentioned earlier is the physical plane. The next level up is the djinn plane also mentioned earlier (and which we will come back to in chapter 21 and appendix D). The forms that make up that plane are djinn thought-forms. Beings who dwell on the djinn plane are aware of those forms just as we are aware of physical objects on our plane. The physical plane is lower than the djinn plane in that all physical objects and all our thoughts have underlying djinn thought-forms; and if those thought-forms ceased to exist, so would the related physical object or thought.

THE ANGELIC PLANE

The highest plane of existence—the most abstract, etheric, and emotionally based of the planes—is the angelic. It is the first step down from the structureless unity of Pure Intelligence and Pure Emotion. Consequently, the angelic plane has very little structure and action compared to our world. It is populated by angelic beings, individual centers of intelligence, awareness, and particularly emotion, although the individuation is not nearly so pronounced as it is in our physical world. Most of the beings there have only general inclinations, with few means to respond to them.

Because the angelic plane provides the first step from nonexistence to existence, its forms are not sharp, concrete, or richly detailed like our third-level physical forms; instead, they are indistinct, less specific and individualized, without great variety. They are akin to light. Sunsets, certain landscapes lighted in a particular way, the face of a beautiful child, and occasionally (actually, rarely) visual works of art trigger dim memories of this realm. The forms of the angelic realm are also akin to music, and some ethereal—actually, angelic—music can trigger memories of this plane, just as light can. The angelic has been described as a realm in which all the inhabitants—angels—spend their time in song, singing praises to { }. The angelic plane is a place of great austerity compared to the djinn and the physical planes. It is sometimes called the land of ice and snow to show its purity and stillness.

There is a first means or accommodation for intelligence on the angelic plane, but it is nebulous, not at all like the myriad interlocking details we have on the physical plane. The angelic is, however, a plane of surpassing emotional beauty. The traces of the angelic plane that one sees in human beings are the higher emotions—especially the higher forms of love and appreciation of beauty in all its forms. There is also a certain quality or mix of qualities, unique to each person, that we have brought with us from the angelic plane. Each of us has buried deep within our own individual "song"—like the blue whale—a song that expresses our most essential self, inherited from the angelic plane.

The Power of the Angelic Plane. In spite of its lack of the detailed intelligence and knowledge we are familiar with on the physical plane, there are beings of great power that dwell on the angelic plane. If one has great strength of will and if one can become clearly aware on the angelic plane, either while alive or after death (very, very few reach this state), the possibilities are unfathomable. For even though events there proceed at a glacial pace, there is great leverage. A small movement by a Great Being on the angelic plane can cause enormous changes on the djinn and physical planes because the angelic lies above the djinn and physical, and therefore determines in broad outline what happens on the two lower planes.

We can gain some appreciation of the power of the angelic plane from Rumi's description of Muhammad's encounter with Gabriel, one of the most powerful of angelic beings.

Muhammad, in the presence of Gabriel,
    "Friend, let me see you as you really are. Let me look
as an interested observer looks at his interest."

"You could not endure it. The sense of sight

is too weak to take in this reality."

"But show yourself

anyway, that I can understand what may not be known

with the senses."

Muhammad persisted in his request,

and Gabriel revealed a single feather

that reached from the East to the West,

a glimpse that would have instantly crumbled

to powder a mountain range.

Muhammad stared, senseless.

THE ATTRIBUTES OR QUALITIES OF EXISTENCE

When { } created that which is, She-He had in mind certain qualities upon which to base existence. These qualities, which come into existence on the angelic plane, are the first step away from the unity of the original longing. The forms of existence, first the angelic and then the djinn and physical, were brought into being partly to provide ways of developing these qualities, ways of making them successively more specific and concrete.

Each human being has his or her own individual attributes or qualities. Each of the various past and present civilizations of the earth has had certain defining attributes—wisdom, compassion, material wealth, as well as other less positive qualities. And each species of animal or plant also carries certain qualities—lilacs and remembrance, mountain lions and ferocious grace—although we do not always have specific names for them. (That is why the extinction of a species feels like such a loss; a quality of existence has been lost.)

The major qualities that pertain to human beings have been given as sacred names of the One who brought existence into being. In the Quran, for example, there are ninety-nine names for Allah, and there are other names to be found in other sacred writings.[1] Some of the Quranic names are associated with positive qualities—the compassionate, the beautiful, the majestic, the one with insight; some are simply more descriptive of existence—the hidden, the manifest, the subtle, the energy of life, the light of being; some are descriptive of humanlike qualities—the administrator, the forgiver, the friend, the compeller; and some appear to be more negative—the avenger, the enforcer, the taker of life—although these, too, are, at least for now, a necessary part of our existence.

Each of the Great Beings—the historical prophets and others—epitomized one or more of these qualities. One might think of Abraham and power; Jesus and surrendering love; Buddha and insight; Joseph and beauty of being; Solomon and insight, poetic beauty, and mastery; Mary and total sympathy, beauty, and light; Muhammad and surrender to the will of { }, and thereby the carrier of the power of { }.

Each of us has one or two qualities as our dominant attributes, although they may not be qualities that have as specific a description as those just mentioned. Some mystics say we should develop a balance of qualities, but most say it is better to concentrate on only a few. It is the hope of { } that we will develop our qualities as far as we are able.

HIERARCHY

We now have three planes—the angelic, the djinn, and the physical—(there are no other planes)—that stand in a hierarchical relationship to each other, with hierarchy used as a device by { } for increasing complexity and the potential for satisfying the goals of existence while avoiding chaos. The forms of the three planes have a hierarchical structure—from more diaphanous on the angelic plane to thoughtlike on the djinn plane to concrete objects of physical existence. Intelligence has a hierarchical structure, being more descriptive and attribute-oriented on the angelic plane and more logical and computerlike on the physical plane. But it is primarily emotion and its hierarchical structure that interests us here.

EMOTION

Pure Intelligence devised the structure of existence, but there is no existence without emotion. Pure Emotion is the force that allows the cosmos to exist, the glue that holds it together. Pure Intelligence is the servant of Pure Emotion (the original longing) just as our intelligence is the servant of our emotions.

Emotions have a hierarchical structure; at each level, just as there is a means or accommodation made for intelligence, so also there is a way for emotion to make itself felt. On the physical plane, for example, mechanisms for emotion are built into the structure of the brain.

Going up the hierarchy, the emotions are successively more subtle but no less strong. Coming down, they are successively more specific and less closely related to the original longing. We are less familiar with the higher emotions because our society teaches us to ignore them. Friendship, intimacy, and creativity are the emotion-words I use to describe the goals of existence, even though they are not entirely accurate, because they are the emotions we are familiar with on this plane.

Emotions play two roles in existence. They are that which motivates us, that which gives us the energy to climb mountains and pursue love; they are that which impels our soul to make its journey, and in the form of feelings, they are also that which tell us whether we are moving toward the goals of existence—friendship-intimacy and creativity—or away from them (for we do indeed have the freedom to move in the wrong direction). The positive emotions of love, compassion, and so on indicate to the person experiencing the emotion that he or she is moving toward the goal (union); while the negative emotions of loneliness, frustration, and so on indicate movement away from the goal (separation). But negative emotions do not necessarily have a negative consequence, for they can act as a signal to spiritually healthy people that something needs to be adjusted in order to move toward the goals of existence. Thus, emotions provide the impetus for our actions, and they are a compass.

Often, though, it is difficult to obtain a clear direction for our actions from the compass of our emotions because there are many levels of emotion and because judgment is needed. Take the primary drive toward friendship, for example. When this is combined with our human weaknesses, it can take the derivative form of concern about others' opinions of us, so the original emotion spawns secondary emotions—the desire to have others think well of us, admire us. You can make the desire for respect and admiration into a journey away from friendship instead of toward it; for example, you can put all your time into getting ahead in the cutthroat world of business without ever forming satisfying friendships. Or, from fear, you can distort the drive for friendship into friendship with a few and enmity toward others.

The same holds for greed, lust, and all the other classic deadly sins; there are just unhealthy, unwise distortions of the original impulses to move toward appreciated creativity and friendship-intimacy. So, we see that because the emotions are complex, we must develop the wisdom to know which ones to follow. This can be done only if we are able to discern our deepest emotions, the ones nearest the goals of existence, and follow those. In the end, we can discern these deepest emotions only by shifting our point of view toward that of { } and away from being focused on narrow gains for our lesser selves.

GIVING UP EMOTIONS?

Some religions teach that we should give up desires and subdue our emotions. I do not agree with this. It is certainly true that lower emotions, when combined with faulty wisdom, can lead to a dismal end; it is true that emotions can entangle our awareness and prevent any perception of a higher plane or purpose; and it is true that it is often better to clip the excesses of emotion—not wallowing in self-pity, for example, at the negative end, and "limiting" our joy to sober ecstasy rather than wild rejoicing at the positive end.

If we give up all our emotions and desires, however, we give up the primary gauge of our experience; we give up an irreplaceable source of motivation—the striving toward joy and ecstasy—and we severely distort the goal of existence, because emotion is inextricably tied to that goal. Thus, we must learn instead to deal intelligently both with the secondary emotions that dominate on the physical plane and with Pure Emotion, that *sine qua non* of existence.

DEATH

The mystics tell us that we still feel emotions after we die; in fact, the emotions intensify. But the emotions of the physical plane can become habits, part of each person's limiting mindset. So if your mindset on this physical plane is driven primarily by anger, your mindset after you die will also be driven by anger. Conversely, if you appreciate beauty here, you will be aware of beauty there; if you are open to love here, you will experience love there.

THE JOURNEY OF THE SOUL

Most of us believe that our existence starts at birth and ends at death, but the mystic knows otherwise. Each of us, each soul in traditional language, makes a long, long journey—angelic to djinn to physical, back to djinn, and back to angelic.

INCARNATION

Before the beginning, before time began, there was no existence and there were no beings; there was just { }. { } was lonely. In response to this, Pure Intelligence, the brilliant, creating part of { }, thought "I will send out rays from myself, rays that will have awareness, discriminating intelligence, long-ing, and freedom to respond to that longing." And as soon as it was thought, it came to be. Each ray was a soul, a separate being, although the separation be-tween beings is less than it seems here on earth. Each of these beings, to ban-ish the loneliness, could be a friend to other beings.

Each of us started out as one of those rays, an angel existing on the angelic plane. We acquired there an affinity for our own individual mix of the quali-ties of existence—beauty, majesty, mastery, and so on. Most of the souls on the angelic plane—entranced by the simple fact that they exist, by the beauty of the plane, and by their nearness to { }—have stayed on that plane; they have not progressed. (That is, most angels are less developed beings than we are.)

But we who are now embodied were too restless, too driven by longing to stay on the angelic plane. We each had a power of being that enabled us to be born into existence on the djinn plane, where beings have more individuation than on the angelic plane, but less than on the physical. We became able to perceive djinn thoughts.

Because of our individual inclinations, each of us became interested in and sensitive to a certain range of djinn thoughts. The interest in particular djinn thoughts was often sparked by communications with other beings on the djinn plane. If those beings had lived on earth and then died, they would have given us general impressions of life on earth, impressions which helped to determine our attitudes here.

As with the angelic plane, many souls continue to live on the djinn plane, entranced by the beauty, complexity, and potential of the djinn thoughts. Again, though, those of us who were more driven, more powerful, and more fortunate moved on to the next plane. We gained the unparalleled privilege of being born into existence on the physical plane, with the accompanying physi-cal body and brain.

ALIVE ON ALL THREE PLANES

Gaining physical existence does not mean we cease to exist on the other planes, though; each human being is able to participate in all the levels of existence. Each of us essentially *is* a Mind—a fragment of Pure Intelligence—with three bodies, three successively more complex "means" for the Mind to use. We each have a brain-body made from the physical forms of this plane. We each have have a djinn body, a coalescence of our own individualized collection of djinn thoughts. And we each have an angelic body, made from the diaphanous forms there. The nonphysical aspects of our selves are in many ways the more essential aspects, "more you than things that have happened to you," as I (and Rumi) said before.

The physical realm—which we each experience only once in this cosmology—is the place of work and great potential gain: a strengthening of will; greater clarity; discriminating wisdom and insight; the development of the qualities of existence; a chance to create new forms, even forms so powerful that we might change the direction of life here on earth; and the experiencing of ever deeper emotions.

In the middle of the journey of the soul, when we have human form, our awareness is typically confined almost entirely to the physical plane, because we bring the attention of the Mind so fully to bear on physical existence. This severely restricts the possibilities for creativity and friendship-intimacy. The goal of the mystic is to greatly expand his or her awareness to all parts of the djinn and even the angelic plane while still alive. This extended, ecstatic awareness is as valuable after death as it is here.

This awareness has an aspect we do not expect. On the physical plane, we appear to be entirely separate beings. But as we expand our awareness to the higher realms of the djinn plane and on to the angelic plane, the separateness between beings diminishes. Think of a tree, with each person's body corresponding to a leaf. The djinn plane corresponds to the stem of the leaf and the twigs. Our consciousness need not be bound by the outline of the leaf (although it usually is), separate from and objectively looking at other leaves; it can extend into the twigs, and from there it can extend subjectively into all the leaves connected to the twigs. In a sense, we can become the other leaves.

The angelic plane corresponds to the branches and the trunk. Our consciousness can extend to these also, so that, even though our outer form is that of a leaf, our consciousness can be nearly identical to that of the whole tree, including the consciousness of each leaf. You can be both leaf and tree. To be both, though, the leaf must give up the strong focus on gains for itself.

Thus, because of these djinn and angelic connections, we are not separate beings. One of the primary goals of the mystic is to become aware that the apparent separation between beings is not real; this awareness is what true intimacy is.

THE RETURN JOURNEY

We do not remain on the physical plane forever; our physical bodies die. At that point, still possessing djinn and angelic bodies, the awareness of each of us, enriched and perhaps burdened by the experiences and attitudes acquired here, returns to the djinn plane. We each exist there for a long while, with the quality of that existence being strongly dependent on how we lived here, on the physical plane. Then, if we have purified our selves—if we do not dwell on our lesser selves and emotions—while we live on the physical plane, and if we continue that process on the djinn plane, we finally return to the beauty of the angelic plane again. Now, instead of being undeveloped beings of little capacity, however, we are magnificent beings of strength, wisdom, and beauty— and very close to { }. We have finished the journey of the soul—although I suspect it is never really finished.

DUALITY, LIFE, COVENANTS

In much of this book, I have treated existence as if it had a sharply delineated dual nature—a physical aspect governed by the mathematics of quantum mechanics and a nonphysical aspect not governed by quantum mechanics. This duality sprang from my initial thought that the wave function of the physical plane was a form that was entirely separate from the djinn thought-forms of the djinn plane, and for many purposes, it is convenient to think in terms of this physical-nonphysical duality. The drawback of this point of view is the puzzling fact that beings who initially exist on the djinn plane can suddenly—at birth or conception or whatever—become physical beings and perceive this other, totally different type of form.

DUALITY

My thought now, however, is that the insistence on a strong duality between djinn and physical forms artificially creates this puzzle. It is simpler and more consistent to assume that the wave function is a specialized kind of djinn thought-form, one with a mathematical nature. This mathematical type of djinn thought-form was brought into existence because it led to a reality that is simpler, more stable, and more sharply defined than the realities in other djinn realms, and these qualities gave this form of existence the potential to be more fruitful in some ways than other forms.

WHAT IS LIFE?

There is a duality in our world that is more apparent than that between the physical and nonphysical worlds, and that is the difference between living and nonliving matter—between storks and stones. What is it that distinguishes living from nonliving matter? Is the matter itself different? In this cosmology, it is not; instead the distinction is that *the physical body of each living being has a nonphysical Mind associated with it.* Why are Minds associated only with living beings rather than with all objects?[1] Because a Mind will only inhabit a physical object that gives it many fruitful quantum *choices* for its actions.

A quartz crystal will not do as the basis for physical life. Why? Because its wave function does not contain sufficiently varied possibilities. It cannot *do* anything; it cannot move, for example. If there were a Mind associated with the quartz crystal, it would not have any interesting choices—corresponding to our thoughts or actions—to make because the quantum branches of a quartz crystal wave function contain no choices.

The same holds for a computer. Although the hardware of the computer is complex, the complexity is of a classical rather than of a quantum nature. For all the many different possibilities inherent in a computer do not coexist together as different branches of the wave function at a given instant; instead, there is essentially only one branch, only one possible future, and thus no choices. (So-called quantum computers may be an exception.)

But when there is a physical object as quantum mechanically complex as that of a cell, the wave function contains many possibilities; the cell can move to the right or left, it can accept or reject foodlike morsels, and so on. So the primary physical attribute a physical object must have in order to be alive—that is, in order to entice a Mind to become associated with it—is that the object must have a sufficiently complex wave function, one that gives the associated Mind many choices.

The purpose of the body is to give the Mind a tool for moving toward the goals of existence—creativity and friendship-intimacy. In the case of the cell, the movement is very limited. In the case of human beings, however, the tool (the brain-body) is incredibly fluid and versatile because of the rich variety of the quantum branch structure of the brain; at any instant, there is a rich infinity of options.

•   •   •

There is another aspect to the definition of life (there are actually several other aspects, including the ability to reproduce, but those are not relevant here), an aspect that has to do with what happens on the djinn plane. Roughly speaking, there is a template on the djinn plane for each form of life here. And there are "operating instructions" on the djinn plane related to the operation (by the associated Mind) of each type of bodily mechanism. These djinn-based templates and operating instructions, as well as the physical forms, evolve over time (see chapter 21 and appendix D).

TENNIS, COVENANTS & THE GAME OF LOVE

We are beings who have "agreed" to subject ourselves to the rules of quantum mechanics. To give this view a more picturesque form, consider the game of tennis. The players of the game agree that, to gain the benefits of play, they will follow certain rules. The rules are related to the court (a rectangle marked off on the ground to delineate the confines of the game) and the net (the barrier).

It is, I believe, the same with existence. The court and the net correspond to the physical laws (quantum mechanics), and the rules and strategies of the game correspond to the psychological laws (brain structure and function) of life on earth. We, each of the souls here, have made a covenant with one another and with { } that we would play the physical universe game. From this point of view, physical existence corresponds simply to a set of agreed-upon restrictions and rules—but wondrous rules, rules that allow us to play the game of love.

THE DJINN PLANE & MYSTICISM

THE REALMS OF THE DJINN PLANE

The distinguishing feature of the djinn plane as a whole is that the forms from which it is constructed are djinn thought-forms. There are simple thought-forms and more complicated thought-forms made up of combinations of the simpler ones. (See appendix D for the idea of atoms of djinn thought-forms from which all other thought-forms are constructed.) There are thought-forms that are closely related to each other, somewhat as our ordinary thoughts of ferns and flowers are related; and there are thought-forms that are less closely related, as are our ordinary thoughts of endive and economics.

The thought-forms that are more closely related are grouped into realms of the djinn plane. Each realm is a separate kind of existence, on a par with our physical existence. You can get some idea of the differences between realms by considering animal life on the physical plane. Think of how different the world appears or feels when perceived by microbes, insects, birds, and humans. The experience of living in the various realms is just as different.

Each realm encompasses a vast range of djinn thought-forms, and there can be many subrealms. Djinn thought-forms in the same subrealm bear more kinship to one another than to the djinn thought-forms in different subrealms. But the djinn thought-forms in different subrealms are not so different as are the djinn thought-forms in different realms.

Each realm corresponds to a form of existence, a means of trying to move toward the goals of existence. And each realm has inhabitants, that is, there are djinn-plane beings in each realm whose Minds focus on the djinn thought-forms of that realm. (If there are no beings whose Minds focus on a particular realm, that realm is not "in existence.") The inhabitants are of three types: There are beings who have never incarnated on earth; there are beings who have lived on earth, and after dying, have come to live in a particular realm; and there are the living mystics who can visit these realms while dwelling on the physical plane.

THE DJINN MIND

Each of the Minds that has progressed farther than the angelic plane has gathered to itself on the djinn plane a collection of djinn thoughts. Or, rather than saying the Mind has gathered djinn thoughts, it is more accurate to say that the Mind has ready access to a collection of djinn thoughts. To use an analogy from my own experience, because of my daily thought habits, I have ready mental access to physics ideas, relatively poor mental access to economic ideas, and virtually no mental access to ideas related to the law.

How did this personal collection of djinn thoughts come about? When the Mind first became aware on the djinn plane, it was interested in—aware of—only a few djinn thoughts. But then it became aware of associated djinn thoughts, djinn thoughts similar to those of its initial interests. By this associative process, the djinn mind acquired a coherent—related, not random—collection of djinn thoughts that it was interested in and had ready access to. This ready-access collection constitutes the memory of the being-Mind on the djinn plane.

A being-Mind resides in that realm in which it focuses its awareness. Most all beings on the djinn plane, including beings who also have physical bodies, reside in—that is, focus their awareness on—a single realm. And, in fact, most reside in a small subrealm of that realm. The reason for this is that Minds get used to and proficient at focusing only in a certain narrow range of djinn thoughts. The mystic seeks to expand that focus.

EXPERIENCE ON EARTH

As I just mentioned, there are three types of beings who dwell on the djinn plane: those who have not yet incarnated, those who currently have a physical body, and those who have died. All three have djinn Minds—the aspect of Mind that perceives djinn thought-forms. Because of the qualities of the djinn Mind—perception, memory, association, abstracting essence, and so on—it can learn. In particular, the djinn Mind of a human being learns a great deal from the experience of physical existence. Thus, the djinn being of a person who has died will be much different after death than it was before birth. (Otherwise, physical existence would not have much point.)

DJINN-PLANE KNOWLEDGE

ORDINARY LIFE

How do or can the djinn realms affect our lives? First, ordinary life. It is not lived strictly within the confines of the physical brain. As I explain in appendix D, the djinn Mind plays an integral role in our decision-making, so none of us are strangers to its use. But we are usually not aware of using it; that requires a different level of awareness. Nor—a gross understatement—do we take full advantage of it. We usually settle for access to a small sub-subrealm of the human subrealm of the djinn plane. This limited access means that the brain thoughts we can have are limited in scope.

Further, each human Mind resides in a slightly different cubicle of the human subrealm. That means our thoughts, which have their basis in djinn thoughts, have a restricted range. This contributes to our lack of understanding and appreciation of others' points of view, because the djinn thoughts I have ready access to are different from those you have ready access to. Conversely, we usually feel "good vibes" from someone if we feel (intuit) that that person is sensitive to the range of djinn thoughts we are sensitive to.

INTUITION

Intuition is knowing by other than ordinary sensory means. It is information gotten from the djinn plane through the djinn Mind. We already use intuitive djinn information more than we realize. When you meet someone, you have been led to believe that your opinions of that person come solely from your observations and analysis of his or her conversation and body language. But djinn information augments the information you perceive physically, especially if you relax your rigid attention to brain-based thoughts.

There is an interesting phenomenon called blindsight that offers some insight into intuition.[1] It sometimes happens, through accidents, that the primary visual cortex (area 17) of the brain is destroyed, but the retina stays intact. People with this disability have no conscious knowledge of sight. If differently shaped objects are put in their field of vision, though, and they are asked to guess the shapes, they will be correct a large percentage of the time! What happens is that there is a secondary optical pathway that transmits visual information to the brain, but doesn't traverse that part (or process) of the brain that makes this information conscious, so the person doesn't know that he or she knows. Nevertheless, it is available information.

In the same way, intuitive djinn information is available, but it does not surface in the consciousness of most people. The trick is either to find ways of making it accessible, even though it is not consciously known or, preferably, to perform practices that train you to become consciously aware on the djinn plane.

MIND READING

We all read minds to some extent, but most of us are not aware of it and do not cultivate this ability. It can, however, be cultivated. The basis for mind reading is that we each have a djinn Mind, and our djinn Mind can telepathically perceive the contents of another's djinn Mind. That content is closely related to what the other person is consciously thinking. Thus, because mind reading proceeds via the djinn realms, the way to cultivate it is the same as for other djinn-related skills; we must learn how to gain access to djinn knowledge.

GENIUS

The djinn plane has many specialized subrealms. A genius is someone who, through natural inclination or hard work, is able to tap into these niches. Mozart had ready access to the music subrealm—not to specific compositions, but to the principles and goals; Cezanne to the visual arts subrealm; Einstein to the structure-of-the-physical-world subrealm, and so on. But these geniuses were typically not aware of the vast possibilities inherent in mysticism, so they didn't expand their area of conscious perception in the djinn plane, as a mystic does.

RANGE OF AWARENESS & PRACTICES

It is useful to think of our range of awareness from the point of view of djinn thoughts. The awareness of an ordinary human being is restricted to a very small corner of the human subrealm of the djinn plane. The practices of the mystics seek to widen the range of that awareness, for we cannot fully appreciate the symphony of existence until we can hear the full range of the orchestra. The neutral practices discussed in part 5 of this book make us experientially aware that we are perceiving in a very narrow range. Other practices in part 5 seek to expand the range.

SHELDRAKE'S MORPHOGENIC FIELDS

Rupert Sheldrake[2] has put forth the concept that once an idea has been given sufficient form, even though it may not have been explicitly stated on the physical plane, that idea is much more readily accessible to others. This concept, which Sheldrake called morphogenic fields, was suggested by the near-simultaneous discovery of many ideas in science and by the hundredth monkey phenomenon.[3] Its theoretical underpinning in the science of the djinn plane would be as follows:

Not all possible combinations of djinn thought-forms exist at any one time. Fruitful, worthwhile combinations of djinn thought-forms can be gathered and tied together into a unified whole—a macro (see appendix D)—by one person. If the power of that person's focus of awareness is strong enough, this unified whole is brought into being on the djinn plane and becomes accessible to others.

Take the theory of calculus, for example, which was developed in the seventeenth century almost simultaneously by Isaac Newton in England and G. W. Leibnitz in Germany. A certain combination of ideas—algebraic, geometric, and the limiting process for infinitesimally small variations—was brought together in such a way that the result was very fruitful; it opened up vast new realms in mathematics and physics. Before Newton and Leibnitz, that djinn thought-form did not exist as a unit. After they put it together and concentrated on the requisite djinn thought-forms, it did.

Sheldrake's point is that, even if Newton and Leibnitz had not made their discovery known, the djinn thought-form of calculus was "out there," and hence much more readily discoverable by someone else. Or if, say, Newton had discovered it first, that would have made it easier for Liebnitz to discover it, even though Newton had not made the discovery known on the physical plane. Thus, complex djinn thought-forms, some of which are presumably the same as Sheldrake's morphogenic fields, have a beginning. And once begun, they become, so to speak, public property.

THE LIFETIME OF THOUGHTS

There is an important variation of this. Mystics tell us that our personal djinn thoughts—ambitions, desires, and so forth—have a life of their own. Once invoked, they will normally not leave us (even at death!) until they are brought to some kind of fruition, because we continue to focus our attention on them. If you want to drop an outdated obsession, you can take special means to get rid of it. One of these, active disinterest, is to discipline your djinn Mind so it does not put its energy into, or attention on, the djinn thought (and related brain thoughts) in question.

GAINING ACCESS TO THE DJINN PLANE

There are different levels of access to the djinn plane and different methods of gaining access. Consider the different levels first.

The less deep ones have to do with gaining intuitive information related to the physical plane, information that is relevant to daily life. Will it rain this afternoon? Which college should my daughter attend? What insight do I need to solve this mathematics problem? The deeper levels of access have less immediate relevance to daily life; they are a more direct way of seeing into the djinn realms for the beauty and power of those realms.

The methods for gaining access to the djinn realms can be roughly divided into two classes. In the first class, you perceive the djinn plane in a way that is analogous to blindsight; you get the information, but it doesn't seem to come through conscious processes. The second class of methods seeks more direct, conscious awareness of the djinn plane and events there.

Consider methods of gaining the first kind of djinn knowledge. As a starting point, I would repeat that we all employ the djinn Mind all the time—in operating the body, and all our other mundane day-to-day tasks. The problem with gaining clear access to intuition is that we get used to paying attention to only certain, very restricted types of djinn thought-forms. And so we think that gaining access to the other, clairvoyant types is supernatural. It isn't—but it is supraphysical. There is, however, a certain amount of learning that is necessary in order to use the less familiar types of djinn thoughts.

The first step in that learning is to gain some stillness and clarity by performing practices such as those of chapters 23–25. Second, you must learn to trust your intuitive abilities. You can begin to pay attention to your intuition to see if you can discern the feel of correct information. As an example, intuition sometimes feels like a non sequitur, rather than like a logical thought; or, it can feel obviously correct.

Third, there are circumstances in which intuitive information is more readily available: during light concentration (where you are thinking freely, not concentrating intensely); or reverie; or a hot bath; or the state just before you fall asleep; or while you're dreaming.

Fourth, some people use devices such as Tarot cards. The idea is that we can establish special circumstances under which we become more fluent at the djinn-mind-to-physical-mind transfer. The essentially random distribution of the Tarot cards allows us to bring to djinn thoughts to the surface—to the conscious, physical mind. It creates a special circumstance in which we have become more skilled at bringing back the djinn thought. When we become more familiar with and skilled at the process, we are able to dispense with the cards.

The second class of methods cultivates a more deliberate, conscious, controlled perception in the djinn plane. Again, the basis is to gain stillness and clarity by performing practices like those in chapters 23–25. Then there is a class of practices that more directly facilitates this learning. These could be described as the cultivation of creative imagination. Many of the visualizing practices—visualizing landscapes of light or the peaceful and wrathful deities of Tibetan Buddhism, for example—fall into this category.

The idea of creating special circumstances also applies to the second class of methods. The use of a mantra, or prayer beads, for example, serves to create a familiar setting in which, because of associations built up over the lifetime of the practice, we are more receptive to djinn thoughts. A sacred chant serves the same purpose.

ENLIGHTENMENT

Enlightenment is an awakening, sometimes sudden, to conscious perception in many of the realms of the djinn plane. There is, however, not just one sudden perception of the whole of the djinn and angelic realms. There are levels of enlightenment, corresponding to how high we can perceive in the djinn and angelic planes.

THOSE WHO HAVE ACCESS TO THE DJINN REALMS

There are lower, less refined, less subtle, and higher, more refined, more subtle realms of the djinn plane, with the higher realms taking on more and more of the flavor of the angelic plane. There are also realms closer to the human realm and farther from the human realm. Different mystics have access to different realms and subrealms.

PSYCHICS

Without doubt, there is a good deal of fraud in this field, but there are also true psychics. They have partly mastered perception in those subrealms of the djinn plane where the djinn thoughts are quite near the ones employed in the interpretation and selection of our physical-brain thoughts. Most psychics stay stuck there, instead of learning to perceive the more subtle realms. There are several reasons for this: They are fascinated by the psychic subrealm; they are using that subrealm for itself, rather than thinking of it as part of a vast territory; they may not know of the existence of other realms and subrealms; and they may not have been exposed to techniques whereby they can learn to perceive the successively higher realms.

HEALERS & HEALING

It seems likely that there are many diseases that originate on the djinn plane. That is, there are djinn thought-forms (worrylike or fearlike thoughts, negative views of one's body, discouragement with life) that have an impact on physical health. If this is so, then treatment and the healing process must involve the djinn plane. Thus, many healing techniques—body work, acupuncture, even some AMA procedures—may, at least in part, be devices to get both the healer's and the patient's minds tuned in to the appropriate part of the djinn plane. I am not saying, of course, that all illness should be treated exclusively by djinn methods, but there is certainly a connection between health and the djinn plane.

MYSTICAL TEACHERS

Authentic mystical teachers have wide-ranging, accurate perception on the djinn plane. They perceive not only in the human subrealm, but also in the higher, more subtle realms. For our purposes, the relevant question is what they perceive in their students. Each of us has a djinn Mind that is just as individualized as his or her earthly personality. We each have our strengths and weaknesses on the djinn plane, and closer connections to some realms than to others. Mystical teachers can accurately perceive these features of a student's djinn Mind; they can perceive a student's wonderful qualities and potential (they can perceive the djinn features in everyone, but their close association with the student aids the process). And they can perceive what it is that blocks the student from realizing her or his potential.

Their craft is to devise practices that strengthen the student's awareness of his or her djinn (and angelic) Mind and that remove the blockages. This process takes a long time because we are so attached to our habitual way of viewing existence. Sometimes the full fruition of the student's and the teacher's work—freedom in the djinn and angelic planes—does not come until after the student's death.

Not all teaching is in the obvious form of giving practices. Sometimes the teacher is teaching directly to the djinn Mind of the student, who may even be unaware of it. This type of teaching often occurs during initiations, retreats, and dreaming. This direct, djinn-level teaching can have a profound effect when, at the same time, the student performs his or her practices. Further, the direct teacher-student transmission gives the student special access to the djinn realms that the teacher knows well; and not only the teacher's djinn realms, but also those of the teacher's teacher, and so on. This chain of transmission shows the importance of a connection with an ancient mystical tradition.

As I have said before, finding a good teacher is essential.

GREAT BEINGS

There are Great Beings in every religious and mystical tradition. Many of them are great mystics who have died: the Jewish prophets; Jesus, Mary, and the Christian mystics; Muhammad and the Islamic and Sufi mystics; Buddha and Padmasambhava; Krishna; as well as many others who the major traditions don't mention.

These beings exist on the djinn and angelic planes. They have gained great strength and insight, and are familiar with all the higher realms. It is possible, and rewarding beyond measure, to communicate or commune with these beings.

For some, they act as teachers when there is no suitable living teacher available. For many mystics, the goal is communion with Great Beings, or even { }, rather than insight into the nature of existence.

The question is how to gain access to these Beings. First, the usual rules governing access to the djinn plane apply; the mind must be still and open enough so the cares and interests of this physical life don't block out the djinn thoughts. Second, you must somehow direct your attention toward these Beings. Sometimes historical facts are enough to get you started. Sometimes visualization can help. Sometimes these Beings have left behind chants that are useful in "calling" them. There is often such power in their name. Sometimes, very little direct information or technique is needed. And in the case of Qwaja Khdr, the green dervish of the Sufi-Islamic tradition, it is sheer, desperate longing that calls him.

ZEITGEIST

Each age seems to have an overriding idea, or mindset. In ours, I would say that it is materialism, including both the denial of the nonphysical and the view of human beings as essentially economic animals. This zeitgeist, the mystics tell us, has its origin in the djinn plane. That is, at a given time in history, the djinn thought-forms of humanity in general are limited to a small subrealm of the human realm of the djinn plane. Why are they so limited? The reason, I think, is that once a certain number of people have their consciousness strongly concentrated on access to a set of djinn thought-forms, these become much more readily available to, and in fact they are almost forced upon, others.

This raises the more general question of how much our thoughts are determined by influences from the djinn plane. Many mystics say that restrictive djinn influences severely circumscribe the mindset of all persons, except for those who have, through mystical training, freed themselves of this influence.

DEATH

One of the most relevant reasons to study and practice mysticism is that when you die, you retain your djinn Mind and your existence on the djinn plane. Thus, knowledge of the djinn realms can take away the sting of death—that false sense that you are going out of existence.

What is it like after death? Consider first the time near death. After you die, it may take some time for you to simply become aware that you are still aware, that you have not gone out of existence. (It takes time because you are learning how to perceive through a different kind of consciousness.) In addition, there are factors surrounding your death that have an influence, in the short term, on your experience after death. Basically, it is best (but not essential) to die in relatively calm surroundings, with those around you not overemphasizing their grief.

When we take a larger view, the way in which you have lived your life has a much more profound effect on your djinn existence after death than do the circumstances surrounding your death. If you have lived your life in an undisciplined careless way, events on the djinn plane will seem to happen willy-nilly, very rapidly, much like a frantic dream over which you have no control. Your will will not be effective there. In addition, the negative attributes—fear, anger, self-centeredness—you have indulged in during your life here, on the physical plane, will come back to haunt you even more strongly in the djinn realms.

What is to be done? First, those who have been more selfless here will fare better there. This is not justice being meted out. It is simply a natural law related to the structure of your djinn Mind at the time of death, for a self-centered orientation automatically ensures that your Mind cannot focus on the higher, more beautiful realms. You will have learned to focus your Mind only on lower, less beautiful subrealms. To be able to see higher, you must unlearn that focus.

Second, if you wish to avoid experiencing the djinn realms as a kind of hell, and if you wish to progress—after you die, and hopefully before—to the higher, more heavenlike djinn realms, it is prudent to study and practice mysticism here. For it is far easier to educate your djinn Mind *here*—to give it mastery, insight, an appropriate selflessness, an appreciation of beauty—than it is after death. Without this djinn Mind awareness here, it is nearly impossible to take advantage of the potential of the djinn plane. With it, because your djinn Mind is prepared, you are able to perceive to the farthest reaches of existence; and there is surpassing beauty there.

PART 5

PRACTICES

PRELIMINARIES TO THE PRACTICES

In parts 1 and 4, I outlined the conceptual point of view from which the mystic sees existence. This theoretical knowledge of the nonphysical levels is like a map: although useful and interesting, it is not nearly so rewarding as direct experience. Because of the orientation of our society, however, we do not grow up in a context where we naturally experience the nonphysical planes directly. Thus, almost everyone in Western society needs techniques to (re)establish contact with the nonphysical aspects of existence.

For this reason, I will give here basic information about mystical practices, the purpose of which is to make the nonphysical planes an experiential reality, not just a conceptual scheme. The underlying premises are: that each human being has the potential to be conscious of a much vaster range of existence—a range that includes the realms of the djinn and angelic planes—than is the norm in our society; that it is rewarding in the extreme, both here and after death, to be able to perceive and function in those realms; that we can all learn how to do so (although some find the learning more difficult than others, and many do not care to learn); and that the goals of existence can be truly fulfilled only through mystical development.

You can learn these methods best from a personal teacher, one who sees on the other levels, and sees well enough to know which techniques are best for you at each stage. If there is no suitable teacher readily available to you, there is still a good deal you can learn from a book.

You can learn of the plausibility of the existence of other realms. You can learn of the multilevel nature of human beings and why we are normally unaware of this within ourselves. You can learn of a range of practices designed to open your perception on these other levels. And, through an understanding of how these practices work and what they are designed to accomplish, you can learn how to use them to good effect. You can also become aware that there is a larger community of seekers, and this sense of connection can make the journey more joyful. Joy and connection to others, in fact, are central to the quest.

Before explaining these techniques, however, I should warn you that the completion of the process initiated by performing these processes normally takes a long time, for you are retraining your Mind-brain. Keep in mind all the steps necessary to become an accomplished violinist, neurosurgeon, or dancer. There are things you must *do* in order to learn, and there are stages you must pass through.

The process may be compared to a journey. It is long, but each stage brings its own interest and satisfaction. And you may find after you have been on this journey for a while that there is nothing worth doing in life besides this traveling. These techniques and others like them are the only path to the place we are trying to find.

In the end
one tires of everything
except heart's desiring,
soul's journeying.

RUMI

GENERAL OBSERVATIONS ON PRACTICES

GOALS

As I have said, the purpose of the practices is to make the nonphysical planes an experiential reality, but the purpose can be expressed in different ways, with different emphases. First, the reason mystics developed practices and aspiring mystics do them is that they wish to perceive[1] on the other planes. Second, aspiring mystics need to develop the ability to *do*. You need to develop certain qualities—mastery, insight, beauty of spirit, a fine discriminating wisdom, empathy, the art of accomplishment—that are used in furthering the goal of existence, and the practices aid this development. Third, the practices help you to *feel* the deeper emotions, and they help you to feel the interconnection between beings on both the physical and the nonphysical planes. Finally, the goals of the practices are to help us perceive, act, and feel from the point of view of { }. We cannot fully do this, of course, because we are still partly leaf rather than fully tree (chapter 19), but our perspectives can become infinitely more vast than our usual narrow focus on our small wants.

SELECTION & LEVEL OF PRACTICES

There are thousands of practices and variations. I will give a sampling of practices that illustrate the basic principles and are effective in their own right. (I have omitted many valid practices because I have no personal experience with them.) Some of these practices may appear to be quite simple (at least to describe, if not to do). But none of them are for beginners only; they are useful up to a fairly advanced stage. If you perform these practices with your full attention on them, they will carry you quite far along the mystical path.

When learning these practices, it is useful to keep in mind that you *are* a Mind, with three levels to your existence. This gives a warranted optimism to your practice. You simply haven't yet got the knack of consciously perceiving on the higher planes, even though you have all the faculties for doing so.

BEHIND THE NET

In order to appreciate the situation of the average human being with respect to perception in the other realms, it is useful to give an analogy. Imagine a net in front of you. A movie is being projected onto this net, a picture that is always in motion. The scenes from this movie often have no great beauty, but your emotions are tied to what happens there; the story projected onto the net creates a tension and thereby claims all your attention.

But the net is not all there is. Behind the net are beautiful scenes—mountain streams, orchards, vistas peopled with incredible beings—scenes that are capable of evoking high, powerful emotions, scenes that give a richer meaning to life. But you are never aware of these scenes; your attention is so riveted on the content of the movie that you think of the net as solid. It never occurs to you that a change of focus, a relaxing of the tension that holds your attention on the net, would reveal a world beyond.

STRATEGIES OF THE PRACTICES— NEUTRAL & POSITIVE PRACTICES

The exclusive focus on the net, then, is our situation. The practices used to change that focus employ, roughly speaking, two strategies. The first, the neutral strategy, uses methods that relax your very strong focus on the net. The idea behind the neutral strategy is that once you relax the focus of your awareness on this world—specifically on the goings-on of the brain—your Mind will begin to refocus on the other realms of its own accord.

The second, the positive strategy, uses methods that seek to acquaint you with what the world is like beyond the net. The reasoning is that, because the other planes are always there, the possibility of perception on the other planes is always present, even though the perception is currently subconscious, indistinct, or unrecognized. What is needed is a way to draw your attention to the other planes. The positive practices attempt to do this by using a form here in the physical realm that is akin to or in some way analogous to a form in the other realms. The form here might be a sound, or breath. Or it might be the visualization of light or a landscape.

The positive strategies might be compared to learning to find four-leaf clovers by first trying to visualize the pattern they make. They are always there, but your knack for perceiving them needs an initial boost.

PROGRESSION OF PRACTICES

Some of the practices of chapters 23–25 are primarily oriented toward the neutral strategy, some toward the positive strategy, and many take advantage of both strategies. It is usually best to emphasize the neutral practices in the beginning, for two reasons. The first is that the relaxation of your focus on this plane is a necessary prerequisite for other practices; and the second is that if you are not properly prepared, the positive practices can induce spurious brain-based imaginings rather than accurate other-plane perception.

After you have performed the neutral practices for a while and gained some ability to not focus so rigidly on the goings-on of the brain, you can increase the proportion of positive strategy practices. I should note, however, that a teacher may recommend departures from this idealized progression in some cases.

STRATEGIES OF THE PRACTICES— DEVELOPMENT OF THE SELF

The neutral and positive practices are primarily concerned with perception. There are other practices, which I have lumped under the heading of practices to develop the self (or the personality), that are more concerned with being—roughly, the esoteric impression you make on others—and with doing. For example, when you have become a true mystic, you will have much stronger will; you will think many fewer negative thoughts; you will have gained insight, compassion, and balance; and you will see more deeply into the nature of each person. A large part of the proper training of a mystic has to do with this development of the self. In most mystical traditions, these practices (which on the initial level might be called moral precepts or virtues), are taught before any practices are given for perceiving on the other planes, and they continue to be done by aspiring and accomplished mystics alike.

THE FOUR TRADITIONAL PATHS

In addition to the neutral-positive-personality way of categorizing practices, there is a more traditional way of categorizing the different methods of mystical training. These four methods are called yogas—Hatha Yoga, Bhakti Yoga, Raga Yoga, and Mantra Yoga. For our purposes, they are described as follows:

> Hatha Yoga is a path of abstinence, a path where you fast, wear a hair shirt, master the yogic positions as a means of gaining mastery over your lesser self. There is little discussion of Hatha Yoga in this book. Bhakti Yoga is the path of devotion, the path of one lost in God (see chapter 25). Many of the medieval Christian and Sufi saints followed this path—St. Theresa and Rabia, for example. In Raga Yoga, you use the events and circumstances of your everyday life to develop mastery and insight. A good deal of the development of the self is Raga Yoga. And Mantra Yoga is the path of wisdom. Understanding the metaphysics of the previous few chapters at a deep level, as well as much of the development of the self, would be Mantra Yoga.[2]

THIS WORLD & THAT

Finally, a word of advice on the practices, so you do not misuse them. Although the world beyond is very beautiful, it is not meant that your activities in this world are to be abandoned in search or contemplation of the other world. This world is beautiful also, and many creative, worthwhile things can be done here that cannot be done elsewhere. In the general scope of existence, what happens on the physical plane is very significant.

23

THE WATCHING-YOUR-THOUGHTS PRACTICE

Watching your thoughts is the basic neutral practice. As the name implies, the practice is simply to watch your thoughts. Watch passively, as if you had little personal interest in the thoughts and their outcome. Also watch alertly, so you don't get glazed over or drowsy. Sit comfortably (I do not stress posture), close your eyes if you wish, and simply be aware of what is going through your Mind. Don't analyze, or "should" yourself; just watch. If you are not familiar with the practice, try it now for a couple of minutes.

If you are typical, you will find that your brain is quite active. There are so many things your brain feels it (you?) must attend to. Also, if you are typical, your attention was repeatedly pulled away from watching for a moment or longer, and you became engrossed in the thought. That is, your attention became directed toward the content of the thought rather than the watching of the thought, like being engrossed in a movie rather than being aware that it is just a movie.

Why is it so difficult to just watch your thoughts? Your nonphysical Mind (soul) innately has high goals and great potential, but at the time it acquires a physical body, it is naive and without much strength or wisdom. So it takes on, and gets caught up in, all the tribulations of living on earth. Your earthly fears and desires become your Mind's fears and desires, so that your Mind acquires the habit of focusing almost all its awareness on the goings-on of the brain. The activities of the brain become the Mind's universe, just as a gripping movie can become your universe for a time.

When you simply watch your thoughts without getting involved in them, your Mind begins to get the idea that the universe is larger than just your brain's thoughts. You cannot yet perceive behind the (neural) net, but your Mind realizes that it has a choice of whether to focus exclusively on it—or not.

Your Mind needs more than just the idea that it can alter its focus, however. It needs to practice until it is adept at not getting caught by or engrossed in the chain of thought. Your Mind will learn this slowly, for it has had a lifetime of focusing on the vicissitudes of the brain-body.

COMMENTS ON THE PRACTICE

Many of these comments also apply to the breath practices of chapter 24, and to other practices as well.

RULES

There are three general rules that apply to meditation practices. First, they should not be a burden, although you may sometimes have to exert some effort to do them. If a practice becomes irritating, either reduce the time you spend on it, stop altogether for a while, or try a different practice. But don't skip around too much.

Second, meditation practices should not encourage you to withdraw from participation in this world, although they will probably change the manner and tone of your participation.

Third, mystical practices should be a natural part of your life, neither forced nor special. Given our society, this rule may seem a bit odd. Actually, though, it is our modern world—with its unbalanced emphasis on the material, and on continuous, complex thought—that is unnatural. Also, your practices will be more beneficial if there is no spiritual posturing; you should not give the impression that performing practices makes you special. And you should not talk about your practices unless you have a good reason for doing so.

BEGINNER'S MIND

Try not to get frustrated or think negative thoughts about yourself if your Mind gets caught up in your thoughts and forgets to simply watch them. This is an inevitable part of the process. Just begin again, as is implied in the book titled *Zen Mind, Beginner's Mind*.

SCHEDULE

What should the schedule for this practice be like? I recommend no more than twenty minutes a day to begin with, although if you really take to it, and it doesn't cause you to abandon this world, you can do more. Even ten minutes gives your Mind a fair amount of training. You may wish to do this in two five-minute segments. You can gradually increase the time if it doesn't become burdensome. Many people find it helps to perform their practices at the same time each day, but that is not necessary. It is better, however, if you don't skip many days.

BOREDOM

If you get bored, continue into the boredom for a short while, and then stop.

RHYTHM—ACHIEVEMENT

Your practice will often acquire a rhythm. It will seem to go well for a while, and then it will seem to go poorly; you will be enthusiastic and then not enthusiastic. We tend to think we should hurry, but we each have our own individual pace. So normally, you shouldn't push too hard in the not-enthusiastic periods. There is plenty of time for those who conscientiously pursue a mystical path (but time is short for those who don't).

Also, because you are trying to relax your too-narrowly-focused awareness, and because you are not yet fully privy to what constitutes achievement in this area, the usual standards of achievement are not applicable here. Further, because of our individual inclinations, we are each headed toward different regions of the djinn plane, toward different mystical skills, at a different pace, and so comparisons are not useful.

VARIATIONS OF THE PRACTICE

PRACTICES DONE DURING DAILY ACTIVITIES

The watch-your-thoughts practice, as well as many others, can be used for short times throughout the day, while standing, walking, riding the bus, and so forth. You might watch your thoughts for, say two or three breaths several times a day. I recommend this version of the practice. It can be the beginning of the process of having a little space between your thoughts, so that the world is no longer as closed in and limited as it seemed before. The space between thoughts is sometimes referred to as *the void*. When you become more adept, you will realize there is content in the void, but it is djinn and angelic content rather than the usual brain-related content, so it will not feel like content for a while.

KEEPING YOUR MIND IN THE PRESENT

The watch-your-thoughts practice is close to what is meant by the practice, often given in Buddhist traditions, of keeping your Mind in the present.[1]

When your Mind is in the present moment, you are not so concerned about past events or overplanning the future. You are more concerned with being open to and appreciating what is happening at the moment. The difference between the two practices is that when you keep your Mind in the present, it is less about watching your thoughts and more about not getting imprisoned by the associative process and your lesser emotions. This is an excellent neutral practice.

SUBTLETY

Instead of just watching your thoughts, be aware—without getting caught up in them—of any subtle feelings, thoughts, or attitudes that are floating in the background of your awareness. You may not have a word or concept that matches the thoughts and attitudes, but they are important nonetheless. Most people need to give these subtle feelings more attention in their daily lives as well as in meditation, because this is the beginning of intuition, of being more directly aware of the creative, insightful thoughts from the djinn plane.

DETAILS OF THE THOUGHT PROCESS

We can take the subtle observing in a different direction. The watching-your-thoughts practice enables you to observe the thought process in more detail (but just observe, don't analyze). A thought starts out as a pure original idea from the djinn plane, but it is usually an idea that does not fit nicely into the categories you have built up in your brain circuits over your lifetime. As a consequence, because the brain tries to make sense based on previous experience, it superimposes its own meaning on the djinn idea. The superimposed meaning has more to do with the memory categories, fears, and desires etched into the brain structure than with the meaning in the original energy. So almost all the wonderful creative energy and ideas that come to your Mind get shunted into your habitual ruts. Geniuses and mystics have found ways to take advantage of the originality in the djinn thoughts.

THE "PULLING" EFFECT ON THOUGHTS

The watching-your-thoughts practice is a good way to observe the pulling or channeling effect of your brain's functions on your attention. Even when you are trying to just watch your thoughts, there is a strong emotional pull, generated by your fears and desires, toward becoming immersed in the content of your thoughts and forgetting to just watch them.

It is not the brain chatter itself that pulls you away from watching your thoughts; it is the Mind *paying attention to* the brain chatter. The diversion of attention is caused by your motivations. It is not the active brain that is the problem, but rather that your Mind has given a high priority to paying attention to the topics your brain keeps dwelling on. A variation of the practice is to be aware of the motivations that are causing you to pay undue attention to the contents of your thoughts when you are merely trying to watch them. Don't dwell on the motivations; just be aware of them.

Some mystical teachers recommend that you try to find the historical roots of these fears and desires, but many Sufis (and the Dalai Lama) say it is counterproductive to dwell for long on those roots, for that focuses your attention too much on your lower self.

RELEASING PRESSURE & CREATIVITY

The Mind-brain has restrictive preconceptions of where to look for solutions to the problems we all encounter in everyday life, even those we may not recognize as problems. This channels the search for solutions, often in unproductive directions. When you first sit down to start the practice, you take many of these channeling pressures or tensions off your Mind-brain. This often unleashes a flood of creative ideas. To capture these, you may wish to have pencil and paper at hand, but pay attention to these thoughts only for a couple of minutes. After that, politely tell your Mind-brain that its ideas will have to wait; there is something more important to do.

THE PRACTICE & BRAIN FUNCTIONS

The watch-your-thoughts practice is related to several of the brain functions mentioned in part 3 and chapter 28. It teaches something about control of awareness. You can clearly observe the pull of thought-preferences (the micro-emotions of chapter 17) on your attention. You can see how the associative process automatically carries the chain of thoughts from one set of memory categories to another. By becoming aware of these processes, you can lessen their mechanistic channeling of your awareness.

To try this and see its effects, suppose, by making an effort, you keep your mind on visualizing a pyramid, or on a chant, for half an hour (both of these are excellent practices). What happens? Often, your mind becomes clearer; it seems like less effort is needed to accomplish ordinary things; you are both more relaxed and more energized. The reason for these effects is that you have, for the time being, gotten rid of unwanted mechanistic processes, the ruts and frictions, in your Mind and brain.

RHYTHM OF THOUGHT ENERGY—THE GAP BETWEEN THOUGHTS

When you watch your thoughts, you will gradually become aware that there is a certain rhythm to those thoughts. An energy arrives from somewhere (the djinn plane) and triggers a chain of associated thoughts. This energy then dies down, and there is a gap in the activity of your brain until the next surge of energy arrives. (This gap is essentially the same as the space between thoughts I mentioned earlier.) It is good to pay attention to that gap between thoughts, for you are closer to the other realms there than you are when your Mind is engrossed in the brain's chatter.

ALERTNESS WITHOUT THOUGHTS

The watching-your-thoughts practice can lead to interesting results if you continue it for a while—five to thirty minutes, depending on the state of your Mind-brain that particular day. Your Mind is passively but alertly watching the thoughts instead of being caught up in them and being concerned about them. Because of the passive alertness, the Mind doesn't feed energy into the brain's thought generator (the associative process plus the attention mechanisms), so very few thoughts will arise.

This is a good state to be in. Alertness without thoughts shows your Mind that it is more than thoughts and sensory perceptions. It is an excellent technique for preparing your Mind to perceive in other realms. For if you are not in this state, if your Mind is always interrupting its focus elsewhere to become involved in the brain's chatter, then your perception of other realms will be, at best, fragmentary.

> There is a way between voice and presence
> where information flows.
> In disciplined silence it opens.
> With wandering talk it closes.
>
> RUMI

This state with very few brain thoughts can be a welcome one. Because the Mind gets tired of always paying attention to the brain, this break can feel cool and soothing, like water. (This is related to the function of deep sleep.) This silence—which is an absence of brain chatter; there can actually be a good deal happening on the djinn and angelic planes—has been appreciated by all mystics.

STOPPING THE THOUGHTS

In the watching-your-thoughts method, the thoughts die out from lack of any attentional energy being put into them. There is also another way of stopping your thoughts which you may run across in your reading. If you watch your thoughts very closely, you will find that the quick perception of the root of a thought often stops the thought from taking its usual course, that is, from triggering an associational chain of thoughts. This shades over into another practice, that of stopping your thoughts by force of will. I do not recommend this practice unless it is done under the guidance of a teacher, for it focuses your attention in the wrong place—on your brain thoughts—instead of on what is *behind* the brain thoughts.

THE PAYOFF

What is the payoff for this and other practices? The long-term payoff is clear perception on the other planes. The more immediate payoffs are a relaxation of tensions, increased freedom and fluidity of thought, a higher level of creativity, more accurate intuition, and an enhanced appreciation of beauty. Not at every moment, of course, but there will be times when the world seems fresh and interesting, not so jammed up with planning, and "shoulds," when the wind or the light or the song of a bird will seem magical.

24

BREATH, MUSIC & THE CHAKRAS

The word *spirit* comes from the Latin *spiritus,* which means breath. The modern American Sufi master, Samuel L. Lewis, has emphasized this connection between breath and spirit by saying that the Bible can be profitably read by substituting the word *breath* for the word *God* throughout. And in our symbology, { } can be interpreted as indicating the archetypal breath, with { being the outbreath (creating, making manifest) and } being the inbreath (abstracting the essence, the hidden).

Breath can be thought of as a metaphor for { }, but it is a nonconceptual metaphor. To explain, consider the question: Where, or on what, should we focus our awareness so that we are as close as possible to the presence of { }? One answer would be to think of { } as personlike, with superhuman traits.

Although this is often a necessary stage, however, it is not fully satisfactory, because { } is far beyond such concepts, indeed beyond all concepts. The mystics say that focusing on the breath (rather than on a concept) is the best way we have of approaching the presence of { }. The breath conveys what it is possible to convey of { } to our human consciousness, and continued focus on it conveys more and more.

Breath is like a current that runs through all the levels of our existence. Pir Vilayat Inayat Khan, a current Sufi teacher, says:

> As the books, precepts, and doctrines of his religion are important to the follower of a religion, so the study of the breath is important to the mystic. We ordinarily think of the breath as that little air that we feel coming and going through our nostrils; but we do not think of it as that vast current that goes through everything, that current which comes from the Consciousness Pure Intelligence and goes as far as the physical world.[1]

Because of this connection with the deepest levels, breath is a means of focusing energy and awareness and of releasing tensions, those internal blockages that prevent us from accomplishing our purpose. It is a gentle energy, but very, very powerful.

As you perform the breathing practices, remember that you are not just a body. You are a Mind. You are an angelic being who has taken on a djinn body to experience the djinn plane and a physical body to experience the physical plane. Your awareness is much deeper and vaster than you are usually aware of.

CAUTIONS & RECOMMENDATIONS

There are many forms of breathing practices. Some of these involve imposing a rigid rhythm on the breath. Unless you are under the guidance of a qualified teacher, I do not recommend that you perform these practices. It occasionally happens that overindulgence in this type of breathing practice interferes with the normal rhythms of the body.

In all the practices given here, you will breathe in your normal rhythm, or perhaps a little more deeply, a little more from the belly region than usual, with good posture. For most of the practices, keep your breath and your focus refined and gentle. Unless you are a longtime meditator, a ferocious concentration usually indicates an involvement of the lower self and is therefore less beneficial.

Even if you heed these recommendations, you may become self-conscious about your breathing. This is no threat to your health, but if you don't like it, relax your breathing, or change to another breathing practice. Remember, however, that in the long run, breath is perhaps the most powerful technique or tool there is; so do not be quick to abandon these practices. Attention to breath heals and gives insight on every level.

WATCHING THE BREATH

The simplest breathing practice is to watch the breath. There are a couple of ways to do this. The first is to watch something connected with the breath. You might place your awareness on the breath going in and out the nostrils; or on the rising and falling of the belly. The second method is to simply be aware of your breath, not any particular aspect of it. In either case, gently try not to let your awareness wander. Be aware of the breath continuously, the entire time you are breathing in, the entire time you are breathing out, and at the turning points. Even if there seems to be nothing happening, stay with the awareness.

The practice is sometimes accompanied by counting the breaths—up to ten, and then starting back at one—so you have a check on whether you have wandered. If you lose the count, start over, but don't let the counting distract you; abandon it if it does.

As you get used to the practice, you should put less of your attention directly on the breath; put just enough attention so that you do not become unaware of the breath. The rest of your attention is involved in "internal listening"—being aware in a relaxed way of the many things that are going on just outside the range of ordinary awareness.

. . .

Many of the comments I gave in chapter 23 on watching the thoughts apply here also. My recommendations for time are the same; twenty minutes per day is sufficient, and even ten is beneficial. You may wish to perform more than one practice, such as watching your thoughts, and then watching your breath. In that case, fifteen to twenty minutes altogether is a good amount of time to aim for. You can judge for yourself; don't do so much that it becomes a burden, but do enough so you can feel your state alter a little. You may feel a calmness, or you may become more aware, more focused, less frantic as you relax the overactivity of the brain.

BREATH & THOUGHTS

A variation on this practice is to watch your breath and your thoughts at the same time. One way to do this is to be aware of where in the breathing cycle—inbreath, outbreath, lungs full, lungs empty—thoughts originate. (Mine usually originate just as I am beginning to take in my breath.) Breath and the generation of a new sequence of thoughts are closely intertwined. You may be able to observe this in others by being aware of their breathing during conversation.

BREATH & EVERYDAY LIFE

Watching the breath can also be used for short periods as can watching the thoughts. Simply be aware of your breath for two or three breaths several times a day in the midst of whatever activities you are doing at the time.

When in worldly activity, keep attentive between
the two breaths, and so practicing, in a few days
be born anew.[2]

PAUL REPS

Don't be fooled by the "few days!" Like all spiritual practices, breathing practices may take a lifetime to master; that is, it may take a long time to fully experience that which the breath is a metaphor for. But you will find that a regular
breathing practice will soon help to make space between your thoughts. As you
become more proficient at controlling your attention, the spaces will become
longer. This shows you are beginning to break the strong, habitual focus of
your Mind on the workings of your brain. Watching your breath also helps
both to release tension and to foster creativity.

BREATH & YOUR STATE

One of the interesting things about breath is how sensitive it is to your state. If
you are angry or under tension, the breath will reflect this, usually by becoming
shallower and shorter. A means of releasing tension and even anger is to become aware of your breathing in stressful situations. Simply becoming aware of
your breath will change both its rhythm and your tense state. Breathing more
deeply—from the belly rather than the chest—and more slowly will also help
relieve stress.

Yawning is a semiconscious attempt to use the breath to calm or reenergize
ourselves. Consciously sighing, taking a deeper breath than usual and then ex-
pelling it thoroughly, can also be used to advantage. Paying attention to your
breath during the day is one of the most beneficial practices you can perform.

BREATH & OTHER PEOPLE

Often it is easier to see the connection between breath and emotion in other
people than it is in yourself. In addition, becoming aware of the breath of others

can also bring you intuitive information about them. Many people who do not seem attractive or interesting to the socially trained eye can have a most interesting "being." As you become attuned to their breath, they may remind you of spring days, or children playing, or dramatic music.

A breathing practice that involves others is beneficial because it takes the focus off yourself. One such practice is to imagine breathing in through your solar plexus. Then as you breathe out, imagine that the breath of a person you know, who need not be physically present, is calm, that the breathing is relaxing their constrictive tensions.

CAUTIONS

When you first try this exercise, you will probably find it difficult to maintain a clear attention on the other person for more than a few breaths. It is better if you don't tell others you are performing this practice, and it is better if you are not attached to the effect it has on others.

BREATH & HEALTH

Because of the ability of the breath to focus energy and awareness, it can be useful in healing. Don't expect miracles and then be disappointed. And don't use it as a substitute for proper medical care, but it can help. If you have an area that needs healing, imagine breathing in through that area. Do this clearly and gently for a minute or so.

MUSIC

It is not known how far is the destination,
but so much I know,
that music from afar is coming to my ears.

HAFIZ

Music is breath with form. Because of this connection, and because of its direct connection to the higher emotions, music has a preeminent position in mysticism. Hazrat Inayat Khan was a master of spiritual music and had a profound understanding of its role in mysticism, so I will rely on his words.[3]

MUSIC & LANGUAGE

Music is the language of the soul.
Music is the natural language for scripture.

MUSIC & DEPTH

Music touches the deepest part of man's being.
Music reaches farther than any other impression
from the external world can reach.

What the art of painting cannot clearly suggest, poetry explains in words; but that which even a poet finds difficult to express in poetry is expressed in music. By this I do not only say that music is superior to visual art and poetry, but music excels even religion; for music raises the soul of man even higher than the so-called external forms of religion.

MUSIC & THE LAW OF THE UNIVERSE

Among all the different arts, the art of music has been
specially considered divine, because it is the exact
miniature of the law working through the whole universe.

To me, the unity-diversity of physics—the few equations and the enormous diversity of phenomena they describe—is very much akin to music, where the musical structure unifies all the diverse notes and rhythms.

MUSIC & SPIRITUALITY

To obtain spirituality is to realize that the whole universe is one symphony.

MUSIC & PRACTICES

Meditation prepares, but music is the highest for touching perfection.

What is wonderful about music is that it helps man to concentrate or meditate independently of thought; and therefore music seems to be the bridge over the gulf between form and the formless.

MUSIC IN LIFE

We are bombarded with music in our daily lives, and it has an effect on us. Some music drags me down, makes me feel lethargic and aimless; some music gives me physical energy; and some music lifts my spirit very high. Each type of music, each piece of music, carries with it a certain emotion or state or orientation. It is not necessary to catalog these reactions, or to try to put word-tags on them, but it is good to be aware of your reactions to different types of music.

We benefit greatly from listening to, and participating in if we are able, high music—Sufi chants, Gregorian chants, the best of classical music (including opera), some New Age music, and so on. But I find that listening to too much music, even high music, dulls my appreciation of the music.

CHANTING

There are many mystical practices that use chanting, and these can be quite effective. As with breath practices, they help both to keep your attention from wandering and to remind you of forms on the other planes. Chanting can be used to call or gain access to particular qualities. There are chants associated with certain masters or Great Beings. These can be used to gain access to those Beings and the qualities they embody. Finally, I personally don't find chants performed monotonically very effective, although others certainly do. If the chant comes in a musical form, however, I usually find it very effective indeed.

THE CHAKRAS

The chakras are particular locations in the physical body that act as doorways to nonphysical realms. As with the breath, you might characterize the chakras as physical manifestations of a nonphysical reality. You could say they are, or are closely connected with, the "organs of perception" in the nonphysical realms; or you could say they are in some way the localization on the physical plane of our djinn and angelic bodies.

LOCATION OF THE MAJOR CHAKRAS

There are major chakras and minor chakras. In most mystical systems, there are seven major chakras, located in ascending order as follows:

1. At the base of the spine
2. Just below the navel
3. In the solar plexus
4. In the heart area
5. At the throat (actually, pretty much the whole neck)
6. At the third eye, just above where the extension of the eyebrows would meet
7. The crown chakra, near the center of the top of the head

You can experiment with some of the practices to try and locate your chakras more precisely.

FUNCTIONS OF THE CHAKRAS

I will explain these very briefly here. For more detailed information, you will need to consult a teacher (or learn to pay intuitive attention to your own chakras). The lower two chakras, at the base of the spine and just below the navel, are concerned with the energy of life. The solar plexus is concerned with emotions. The heart, also related to emotions, is the primary chakra that needs to be opened to gain access to the higher realms. The throat chakra is related to communication. And the third eye and crown chakras are related to penetrating insight and wisdom. (If these descriptions seem overly connected to the physiological functions of these regions, for example, throat and communication, the reason might be that the physiology is a physical manifestation of a nonphysical function.)

SOUNDS & CHAKRAS

I will provide here an abbreviated list of sounds related to the various chakras. The short "a" sound, "ah," is connected to the heart chakra. (It is interesting that many of the names of Great Beings end in this sound: Krishna, Shiva, Buddha, Allah, Isa [Jesus], Padmasambhava.) The "u" part of { } (whooo) is connected to the throat chakra. The long "e," as in the Arabic Alim (aleeem), chanted in a high pitch, is connected to the third eye. And "om" is connected to the crown center. When chanting these sounds, place them in the appropriate centers. You can actually make the centers vibrate with the sound.

BREATH & THE CHAKRAS

The average person is unable to gain access to perception on the other planes. The reason for this can be that the chakras do not function as they should; they are under a constrictive tension or are in some way clouded so the perception connected with them is unclear. Because the breath enables us to focus energy and awareness, we can use it to cleanse the chakras, relaxing the restrictive tension.

There are many practices in which the breath and the chakras are connected. I will give a simple, effective one here:

1. Imagine breathing in and out through your solar plexus. Lightly concentrate your attention on that area, thinking somewhere in the back of your mind that you are relaxing tensions there. If you like, you can visualize light coming into or emanating from the solar plexus, a yellow light composed of many very, very fine rays.

2. Do the same for the heart, thinking of relaxing the tensions there. Visualize the light of a beautiful golden sunset color emanating in all directions from the heart on the outbreath.

3. For the throat, imagine very refined emerald green light emanating from the entire neck, especially the throat and the upper back of the neck, near the brain. Think of the throat as connecting the head and heart.

4. For the third eye, imagine a piercing ray of violet light entering (inbreath) and emanating from (outbreath) this area.

5. For the crown chakra, imagine sparkling light like that from ice and snow emanating from the top of the head and forming a fountain of light.

As with other practices, ten to twenty minutes a day is sufficient for this practice alone; or twenty minutes is ample for all your practices combined. Again, as with other practices, just do these with your attention on them and with no expectations. They take time to work their magic.

THE PURIFICATION BREATHS

Purification is clearing the mindsets and emotional pulls and tugs that prevent us from perceiving more clearly and accurately. It is getting rid of the tensions—the "shoulds" and restrictive, biased points of view we accumulate as we grow up—that prevent clear perception. This is what Samuel Lewis was referring to when he said, "Tension is the only sin." If you are visually oriented, you may picture purification as dispelling a cloudiness, like sediment in water, or as breathing out black smoke that contains all the thoughts and attitudes you want to discard. Rumi says of purification:

> Be melting snow.
> Wash yourself of yourself.

The purification breaths as described by Hazrat Inayat Khan are a set of four breaths performed five times each. They can be performed daily, beneficially, in addition to other practices, sitting or standing. The breathing is a little deeper than usual. Before starting, relax by exhaling deeply a couple of times.

1. *The Earth Breath.* Imagine breathing in the magnetism (strength, power) of the earth through the base of the spine. As you breathe in, pull the magnetism and breath up the spine to the level of the heart. As you exhale, breathe your impurities out into the earth. The physical breath is in through the nose, out through the nose.

2. *The Water Breath.* Imagine breathing in through the crown chakra, feeling it open. As you breathe out, imagine purifying water flowing down through your mind and body. In through the nose, out through the mouth.

3. *The Fire Breath.* Breathe in through the solar plexus. This fans a flame at the base of the heart, burning up the dross in your system. Breathe out golden light from your heart in all directions. In through the mouth, out through the nose.

4. *The Air Breath.* As you breathe in, imagine a gentle wind coming from in front of you; and as you breathe out, the wind comes from behind you. This wind moves through the almost entirely empty space between the atoms of your body, purifying it completely; your old self practically disappears. In through the mouth, out through the mouth.

In addition to your daily practices, you may wish to use an abbreviated version of this practice—only one breath for each element instead of five, or just do one of the elements (but not fire!)—whenever you experience something upsetting or tension-producing. You will find this practice helps restore your rhythm and clarity, and it has a settling effect.

FURTHER BREATH-CHAKRA PRACTICES

SOLAR PLEXUS–HEART

This practice is essentially the same as the fire breath but is performed breathing through the nose. Imagine breathing in through the solar plexus and out from the heart. As you breathe in, relax the tensions in the solar plexus area. As you breathe out, relax the tensions of the heart. Release the many bruises, slights, and apparent defeats you no longer need to fret about. There are mountains to climb, visions to see, sublime beings to meet. . . .

THIRD EYE–CROWN CENTER

Breathing through the nose, imagine drawing the breath in through the crown center and send it out through the third eye. Concentrate on these two chakras with a relaxed clarity. You may feel a sense of release or opening of these centers. The third eye and crown centers give access to a fierce, penetrating insight. When these centers are fully developed (which seldom happens), there is more power available than in all the armies and economies of the world.

PRACTICES PERFORMED DURING EVERYDAY LIFE

They say love is patient, but have you ever seen a patient lover?

RUMI

Suppose you decide to accept the ideas that you exist on several planes and your potential is far more vast than the secular world would have you believe. When you pass a certain level of acceptance, you become, as Rumi tells us, impatient. The desire to consciously experience more than the physical plane moves to near the top of your priorities. What then? To go where you want to go, you must change the focus of your Mind's awareness. This is not easily done; it will require you to spend more time in practices than the twenty minutes a day I recommended earlier.

The longer practices come in three forms. You can perform the practices already described or similar ones for longer periods each day, say an hour or more. You can perform practices, or perhaps better, have a certain orientation to your mind, during your everyday life, concurrent with your everyday activities. Or you can go on retreats with a qualified guide, during which you practice intensively for three days or more. In this chapter, we will consider the first possibility only briefly and then concentrate on the second one. I will talk about retreats in chapter 27.

Finally, I do not recommend that you perform the practices of this chapter unless you are reasonably healthy psychologically.

LONG DAILY PRACTICES

Some people do more than an hour of practices each day, practices that are separate from their daily lives. But I have found that it is hard to carve so much time out of every day, and also that this style of practice brings an unwelcome separation between my practices and my daily life. If you have a teacher who recommends this, or if it seems to suit you, this method is fine, but I will not discuss this kind of practice, except for:

PRACTICES AT NIGHT

There is a cheating way to get in longer practices. You can cut down your sleeping time by an hour and perform practices when you wake up at night, but don't rob yourself of deep sleep, because you need that as much as the practices. (It is interesting that during the Middle Ages, people often slept in two segments, separated by an hour or so of reverie.[1]) Breathing practices are excellent at night (I particularly recommend { } on the outbreath), as is the practice of the presence of God (to be explained shortly). I usually perform the practices lying down in bed, although that is not supposed to be good form. Muhammad recommends night practices: "The night is long; don't waste it on sleep." So does Rumi (his italics denote God speaking):

> Don't let someone bewitch you.
> Some people sleep at night.

But not lovers. They sit in the dark
and talk to God, who told David,
Those who sleep all night every night
and claim to be connected to us, they lie.

OTHER SLEEP PRACTICES

As you are going to sleep, or if you wake up in the night, relax. Let go of physical tensions, fears, problems, ambitions, emotions. Just exist. It is very freeing.

You might also suggest to yourself as you are falling asleep that you will remember your dreams; or that you will have some control over the events of your dreams; or that your dreams will give you insight into what you should do in some situation. In interpreting dreams, it is best not to use a book of dream symbols. Instead, look for similarities in structure between the dream and some situation in your life. For example, I dreamed I was a saboteur. My interpretation was that it was time for me to blow up—get rid of—certain aspects of my personality. The rest of this chapter describes practices you can integrate into your daily life.

AWARENESS

APPRECIATING YOUR AWARENESS

You have been given the gift of human awareness. In the cosmic scope of things, that is an exceedingly rare and precious gift, so it would be good to make the best possible use of it.

THE BUSYNESS OF THE MIND

If we are aware of our thoughts during the day, we soon see that there are many things that concern us, and these concerns occupy a great deal of our time. Some of these are obviously genuine, but most of the things your Mind thrashes around on are not really essential or important. There are many,

many things you don't need to think about; running others' lives, fixing things that don't need to be fixed, daydreaming, much of the news in newspapers and on TV, imagined problems and conversations, defending yourself, reviewing old hurts, imagining the future.

When your mind is constantly occupied with all these problems, that is, when there is no space between thought-chains, your Mind-brain is forced to remain in a low-level state of awareness. No breath of freshness can penetrate into your consciousness. This is low-key living, living that makes poor use of the energy, openness, and creativity that are potentially available.

There are two phases to dealing with the misuse of your attention. The first is simply to realize that it is not necessary to spend mental time and energy on most of the things you think about. Life is short, and it is an irredeemable loss to spend it on unnecessary battles, on ticking off mental lists, on solving non-existent problems. There are more essential, engaging, rewarding ways to employ our awareness. The second phase is to perform practices that can change your Mind's habits.

PRACTICES FOR EVERYDAY LIFE

Focusing your attention exclusively on the brain's chatter shuts out an immense area from the Mind's perception. One of the primary reasons for performing practices is to reeducate your Mind so it no longer pays so much attention to the thoughts—firing of neural circuits—of the brain. By integrating practices into your daily life, you allow your Mind to become aware in a less restricted way over an extended period of the day.

THREE WALKING PRACTICES

I will describe three practices designed to break the Mind's habitual focus on the brain's thoughts. A good environment for becoming familiar with these practices, before trying them in the midst of life, is while walking at a leisurely pace in an area where there aren't too many distractions. You don't have to walk outside; pacing inside is good also. You should initially perform these practices for only about twenty minutes, and then gradually increase the time. The reason for this is that they require a fair amount of mental effort in the beginning, and if you try to do them for too long, the effort may make you less enthusiastic about doing them the next day.

Space between Thoughts. In the associative process, there are gaps between thoughts. One chain of thought runs out of energy and ends, there is a slight gap, and then another chain begins. These gaps are normally very short. By becoming aware of them, though, you encourage them and they lengthen, although they may still be short. This puts you less under the sway of the tyranny of thought, of having thoughts circulating incessantly in your brain. Going back to the net analogy of chapter 22, if you are conscious of the space between thoughts, your attention is not always on the content of the picture being projected onto the net. In this way, you begin to reclaim control of your Mind, of your deeper self. Perform this practice for a few days until you get the feel of it.

Awareness of the Breath. This is the same practice as that described in chapter 24, only you perform it while walking rather than sitting. Simply be aware of the breath while you walk. This, too, breaks the habitual focus of the Mind on the brain's thoughts. You might try using these two practices—awareness of the thought-gaps and awareness of the breath—on alternate days, so you can feel the difference between them.

Pure Awareness. The third practice is a little more difficult to describe. You are simply aware of being aware; not aware of any particular thing, but just aware. Your attention-selecting mechanism is not on automatic pilot. You can have this type of awareness while at the same time having awareness in the ordinary sense. For example, you can look at a tree or listen to the wind (an excellent practice in itself) and still be aware of being aware. It is as if a part of your awareness is reserved for checking that you are still aware, not caught in the thought or perception of the wind or the tree. This pure awareness practice carries with it a special kind of alertness, like a tiger looking for prey. You are quite alert during all three practices, in fact, but at the same time, relaxed.

DURING THE DAY

A leisurely walk is always a good time for doing these practices. Once you become familiar with them, however, you can start performing them throughout the day, "in traffic." You need to learn to perform these practices while engaged in all kinds of activities: driving, riding a train, talking, listening, exercising. (However, I find them more difficult to perform when solving problems, learning, or thinking creatively.) I suggest that you aim for about twenty minutes of awareness each day when you start, then you can gradually increase the time.

You may initially find these practices discouraging. Because of our mental habits, it is hard to remember to be aware in the ways suggested. But it may help to be reminded that everyone who has done this—that is, everyone who has sought to become a mystic—has had the same experience. It is not easy. On the other hand, you may find that there is an energy generated by the very difficulty of the practice, akin to the feeling you might get when climbing a mountain.

You may also find it is easy to overdose on any of these practices, especially when first starting. If you find them burdensome, cut back on the time or give them up entirely for a while.

These practices are one way in which modern mysticism differs from the classic yogic withdrawal from society. What we are attempting here—staying in the world and still having a full-blown practice—is both more difficult and more rewarding than what the yogis attempt.

EVERYDAY MINDSET PRACTICES

Both the brain and the Mind develop habits—mindsets. At a lower level, our brains form habitual ways of dealing with the world. At a higher level, our Minds also form habits. They learn to focus in a narrow range, to have a narrow perspective. This restricts the possibilities open to us.

The practices I just described seek to widen your mindset in a general way. Those I will now describe seek to free up your mindset in a more specific and direct way. They open up your narrow view by working on the particular habits of your Mind that restrict you the most. These practices, like most others, are better done under the supervision of a teacher.[2] I have included them because they are important and effective, even necessary at some stages, but if they induce too many negative thoughts, stop them.

EXTERNAL PRACTICE TO REDUCE ANGER

To illustrate this type of practice, suppose that you often get angry (most of us do this more than we realize) and that you have decided this is a habit that wastes your energy and attention, a habit you would rather be without. To start the process of getting rid of anger, choose one hour a day and do not *outwardly* express anger during that time. Do this, at the same time each day, for thirty days.

This practice is difficult: We forget. Or we feel that anger is not really under our control; it is brought about by the events in our lives. But our anger *is* under our control. And we can, with practice, remember. So just stay with the practice for the full thirty days and you will see some progress.

When you are performing the practice, be easy on yourself; do not run yourself down. It is very difficult to break mindsets. Again, if the practice does not agree with you, if it is inducing too many negative thoughts, give it up. There are many other practices to try.

INTERNAL PRACTICE

If you survive the first stage and see some progress, you may wish to try the second stage, which is more internal. The second stage is not to dwell on or pursue *thoughts* of anger. If angry thoughts arise, gently push them aside and choose another chain of thought.

You need to be psychologically healthy to do this internal version, because it can be quite discouraging at first. We feel we do not have that kind of control over our thoughts. Often our anger seems even worse after we start the practice. Gently keep at it: Gentle energy is better than intense effort here, as elsewhere in mystical practices, and a great deal of patience is needed.

This second stage is called a Jihad in Islam—a holy war. It is a war not against an external enemy, but against your lesser self. Getting rid of a restrictive mindset is a major victory in this war.

OTHER RESTRICTIVE MINDSETS

There are many other restrictive mindsets besides anger that can be used in this practice. A sampling would include the following:

- For the external practice or stage 1, speak no ill of others. For the internal practice, or stage 2, neither speak nor think ill of others.
- For stage 1, show no outward signs of self-pity. For stage 2, neither outward signs nor thoughts of self-pity. Simply refuse to follow self-pitying chains of thoughts.
- For stage 1, do nothing outwardly to defend your actions or behavior. For stage 2, do not defend your actions (and thoughts) not even to yourself.
- For this one, which is a continuation of the first one in this list, you need to pay close attention to how others will interpret and feel about your words and actions. Because of this, it is midway between external and internal practices. Do not say or imply anything that would make another person feel bad about her or himself; do not impute blame or engage in sarcasm or biting humor; make no one feel inferior, instruct no one on how best to live his or her life.

Not all emotions associated with these restrictive mindsets are "bad"; anger, for example, can be a source of energy. But they are bad when you indulge in them mindlessly and habitually, that is, when they restrict the range of your Mind's awareness.

There is one other mindset practice. Make a list of the eight or ten major mindsets that determine how you see the world. These may involve how you view others and your relation to them, how you view your own capacities, how you view what is and is not possible in your life, and how you view the nature of existence. See if some of these mindsets are related to fear. Think about how they may limit you, and begin to think about how to get beyond these limitations. It requires courage, but all you have to lose is your uncomfortable comfort and your agitation.

The point of these practices is not to make your life miserable by dwelling on your faults. It is simply that to advance on the mystical path, you need to get rid of restrictive mindsets. Getting rid of just one or two restrictive mindsets is a great advance.

THE PRACTICE OF THE PRESENCE OF GOD

Lo, I am with you always means when you look for God,
God is in the look of your eyes,
in the thought of looking,
nearer to you than yourself,
or things that have happened to you.

RUMI

The practice of being constantly aware of the source and goals of existence during your daily life occurs in every mystical tradition, and for good reason: We cannot rise above a certain level without it. But the flavor of the awareness varies from tradition to tradition and from person to person. A beautiful example of the flavor associated with the bhakti path, the path of devotion, is given in the book, *The Practice of the Presence of God*. This work was compiled from conversations with and letters written by Brother Lawrence, a seventeenth century

Christian monk. The quotes will appeal to those who are naturally bhakti, devotionally oriented, but they may not appeal as much to those who are jnana, more attuned to insight and wisdom (although I am mostly jnana, and I still find this book profoundly affects me). The passages not in quotes are from records kept by vicar M. Beaufort of conversations between him and Brother Lawrence.

> "I keep myself in His presence by simple attentiveness, . . . an habitual, silent and secret conversation of the soul with God."

> As my spiritual life advanced I found formal times for prayer appealed to me less than constant appeals to God, regardless of what task I was performing.

> I was more united to God in my ordinary activities than when I devoted myself to religious activities, which left me with a profound spiritual dryness.

> I must tell you though that during the first ten years I endured great suffering. . .

> Just as I thought I must live out my life beset by these difficulties and anxieties . . . I suddenly found myself changed and my soul, which up till then was always disturbed, experienced a profound interior peace as if it had found its center and a place of peace.

> I am now so accustomed to this divine presence that I receive continual aid from it in all circumstances; for almost thirty years my soul has been filled with interior joys so continual and sometimes so great that to contain them and prevent their outward manifestation, I have resorted to behavior that seems more foolishness than piety.

Brother Lawrence is an example of an ideal. Don't be dismayed if you fall short of his standards!

VARIATIONS OF THE PRACTICE

If you are to advance far along the mystical path *and* remain in this world, then, as I have said, you must have a practice that you can perform during daily life. You should not take this practice on yourself prematurely, and it is best to have a spiritual teacher to monitor the practice. But if you should decide to do such a practice, and if you find that trying to envision the direct presence of { } is too difficult, there are other orientations for your awareness (although the further you progress, the less effective difference there is in the various orientations).

First, as in the previous chapter, you can choose to simply be aware of your breath as much as possible during the day. This is much more effective than it might seem to the rational mind; it establishes a link between you and { }.

Second, you can put a sacred name or phrase on your breath; that is, deliberately at first, and then more and more automatically, you can silently repeat or think of this phrase. One example is *Toward the One* on the inbreath and *United with All* on the outbreath.[3] This is a superb practice because it constantly reminds you both of the unity of existence *(Toward the One)* and of the friendship-intimacy goal of the diversity of existence *(United with All)*. Sufi-Islamic example is Allah on the inbreath, { } on the outbreath (or just { } on the outbreath). Allah signifies the source and goal of existence, while { } evokes intimacy with the mystery hidden in creation. From the Christian tradition, *Kyrie Eleison* (inbreath), *Christe Eleison* (outbreath), *Lord have mercy upon me, Christ have mercy upon me.* And from the Tibetan Buddhist tradition, *Om Mane Padme Hum* (the e's are pronounced like long a's, the a's as in father): *Om,* both the imperfections and the possible perfection of bodily existence; *Mane,* the methods of becoming enlightened; *Padme,* wisdom; and *Hum,* the unity of wisdom, method, and existence.[4]

Third, you can strive to be continuously aware of a Great Being—a Being who can help you in your quest.

Fourth, pay attention to your intuition during the day. Pay intuitive attention to ordinary things—will it snow? Who will win the election? What is that person about to say? And pay intuitive attention to people—try to feel what they are thinking, what their mindset is, what the djinn and angelic aspects of their beings are like. Try not to be attached to success or failure, and do not discuss the results of the practice with others.

Fifth, you can reduce how much you think each day. Become aware that much of your thinking—overplanning, worry, reliving the past, daydreaming—is not really useful and can be done away with. (Of course, there are still many things that need to be thought about, so don't take this to harmful limits.) Shamshir, a twentieth century Norwegian Sufi mystic who was also a high-level defense scientist, allowed himself only two hours a day of thinking in his later years. And Padmasambhava, the extraordinarily powerful Buddhist mystic from the eighth century, went two years without thinking as a part of his training. In fact, all mystics reach a point where they think considerably less than the ordinary modern person because paying undue attention to brain thoughts severely limits the perspective of the Mind.

Finally, after you have performed these practices or something like them for a while, your moment-to-moment practice may become simply paying attention to the everyday world, or rather, paying attention to what is behind the everyday world—to "that which transpires behind that which appears."[5]

Remember that it takes a long time to become proficient in these practices, so be patient and gentle with yourself. Also, you might imagine that the practices will isolate you from others, but this is far off the mark. Much closer to the truth is a remark in the introduction to *The Practice of the Presence of God*. "It is as if we are travelling along spokes on a wheel, and as we draw closer to the center, we draw closer to each other."

THE ART OF THE SELF

Well-makers lead the water; archers bend the bow; carpenters hew a log of wood; wise people fashion themselves.[1]

HAZRAT INAYAT KHAN

How is your Mind to best use its human form in its all-too-temporary existence on this plane? The answer to this question will not be the same for each person, for each of us has different attributes, different inclinations and desires, a different upbringing, and a different perspective. There is no science for finding an answer, because there are so many personal judgments to be made. Instead, the answering of this question is an art, the art of the self.[2] The shaping of the self is the highest art, higher than the visual arts, poetry, or even music, because there is so much potential inherent in the human form.

When we shape ourselves in the mystical tradition, do we all turn out the same? Not at all. We each have a different mix of attributes and desires, and as we progress, those individual attributes are developed and individual desires are harnessed, so that each mystic develops his or her own individual personality (but not in an egotistical way). Think of the differences between the great mystical prophets—Abraham, Solomon, Buddha, Jesus, Muhammad . . .

KNOWING YOURSELF

How do we learn the art of the self? One of the main ways is to know yourself—what your mindset is, what your lower and higher desires are, what emotions you are feeling. An interesting anecdote illustrating this is told by Pir Vilayat Inayat Khan as an illustration of how intuition works. A man came to Pir Vilayat and said he was being falsely accused of setting a fire. Pir Vilayat was quiet for a few moments and then said, "I don't believe you. I think you set the fire." The person then broke down and confessed. How did Pir Vilayat know? He did not know by feeling what the other person was feeling. He knew by how *he* felt; Pir Vilayat felt guilty.

The same thought is expressed in the *Tao Te Ching,* verse 70.

> If you want to know me,
> look inside your heart.

Pir Vilayat knew the other person by knowing himself, by being sensitively aware of his own state. The same knowing of one's self is also the key to knowing { }:

> To know God is not an easy matter,
> until one becomes a knower of one's self.
>
> IBN ARABI, *KERNEL OF THE KERNEL*

So you come to know { }, at least in part, by looking deep within yourself. But this looking inside is tricky. You must be brave and honest with yourself, and that is difficult indeed. And you must be gentle with yourself, for we all have many weaknesses and will never remotely approach perfection.

MINDSETS

One of the things you need to know about yourself is your mindset, your habitual way of looking at the world. To see this, it is often useful to look carefully but not intrusively at the personalities and mindsets of others, for the contrast between them and ourselves can tell us much. Once you know something about your mindset, you can use the techniques of the previous chapter to get rid of a few of the most restrictive emotions. (Eventually, though, you will put less emphasis on "improving" yourself and more emphasis on being aware of the higher realms of existence and the higher beings.)

THE EGO

Each of us tends to think of him- or herself as the center of the universe; what happens to us is all-important. This limited sense of self, the ego, is not bad in itself; it just is. Up to a certain point, it is an indispensable motivator, a necessity for the existence of individual forms. At the same time, it can, and often does, bring us into conflict with the overall goals of existence.

The contrast between the higher goal of friendship-intimacy and the lower goals of the limited self are captured in this poem by Rumi:

TWO WAYS OF RUNNING

A certain man had a jealous wife
and a very, very appealing maidservant.

The wife was careful not to leave them alone,
ever. For six years they were never left
in a room together.

But then one day
at the public bath the wife suddenly remembered
that she'd left her silver washbasin at home.

"Please, go get the basin," she told her maid.

The girl jumped to the task, because she knew
that she would finally get to be alone
with the master. She ran joyfully.

She flew,
and desire took them both so quickly
that they didn't even latch the door. . . .

Meanwhile, the wife back at the bathhouse,
washing her hair said, "What have I done!
I've set the cotton wool on fire!
I've put the ram in with the ewe!"

She washed the clay soap off her hair and ran,
fixing her chador about her as she went . . .

The maid ran for love. The wife ran out of fear
and jealousy. There is a great difference.

The fearful ascetic runs on foot, along the surface.
Lovers move like lightning and wind.

No contest.
Theologians mumble, rumble-dumble,
necessity and free will,
while lover and beloved
pull themselves
into each other.

One might think that the ego vanishes after a certain point on the spiritual path, but that is not exactly true. We still want things for ourselves, but the sense of self becomes broader, so that it includes others. As the Dalai Lama says, we should become wisely selfish rather than foolishly selfish.

ATTRIBUTES

One of the main components in the art of the self is the development of certain attributes or qualities. These are the attributes that { } hopes the free-willed beings of existence will come to exemplify. There are many, many attributes—majesty, compassion, forgiveness, healing, and so on—but I will discuss only four here; mastery, insight, beauty, and, briefly (in chapter 29), friendship. Each of us should try to develop an attribute to the fullest extent possible. It could be one of the classical attributes or a harmonious combination of a few, or even an attribute that has no commonly recognized name or definition. The attribute you emphasize is up to you (and your teacher); it depends on your individual inclinations and aptitudes.

Each of the attributes I have chosen here are associated with a particular orientation to existence: Mastery is associated with the desire to accomplish, insight with the desire to perceive existence and gain wisdom, and beauty with the desire to experience existence. The full development of any one of these qualities also confers something of the others. And it brings us close to what we really desire.

MASTERY OF THE SELF

One of the attributes most necessary for progress on the spiritual journey is the mastery of the self—the ability to make yourself do what needs to be done. Mastery is the harnessing of the freedom of choice that has been given to each being. Most dwellers in the angelic and djinn realms who have not incarnated here lack a strong mastery of the self. It is an attribute that is much more difficult to acquire on those planes than here. There is less to push against, so to speak, on the other planes, and thus less chance to develop mastery. The physical universe is the plane of work, the place where progress is most possible.

Why is self-mastery necessary? To see why, consider its opposite, the absence of willpower. If you are not the master of yourself, you cannot set a course and follow it; you are essentially an automaton, and there is less point to your existence. In this cosmos, where freedom is given but success is not assured, it takes effort—properly directed effort (the "skillful means" of the Buddhists)—to progress toward the goals of existence. The need for appropriate effort is synonymous with the need for mastery.

We also need mastery because, although the human form is a superb vehicle, it is far from perfect. So in addition to striving to achieve the greater goal, we must at the same time deal with all the lesser but necessary survival motivations introduced by having a physical body. To exaggerate a bit, we might say we have to override the lesser goals of physical existence to attain the higher goal. If we are to become the magnificent beings that { } hopes we will become, then mastery of the self is essential.

RESISTANCE TO MASTERY

Mastery of the self, or willpower, is a topic that many people, including myself, are not initially overjoyed to tackle. It evokes memories of failed attempts to gain an iron will and visions of life with no pleasures, but we are not after rigor and asceticism here; we are after mastery where it is needed, and joy, delight, and appreciation where they are appropriate. Also, we have all developed some areas of mastery in our lives and can see that the effort need not be excruciating. So, although it takes effort, the process of mastering the self need not be as distasteful as we sometimes imagine.

TECHNIQUES FOR MASTERY

How do we learn mastery? Here are a few suggestions:

- One sensible approach to the development of mastery is to simply use it. Start in situations where it is not so difficult. Then, as you learn that you really can master yourself, go on to situations where exerting your will seems to be more difficult. For example, if you have trouble getting yourself to jog every day, you could start by just getting dressed to jog each day. Then you could begin to run a little each day, then a little more, and so on.

It is important in this approach to be consistent about carrying out the goals you have set for yourself. You needn't be rigid about attaining every goal, of course; sometimes it is necessary to change goals. But it is better if you attain most of the goals you set for yourself. If you are constantly falling short, lower your aim.

It is also important to realize that the mastery of the self involved in this process is more important than the immediate goal, for the mastery gained in one successful step provides the platform for the next step in mastery of the self. This method is "mastery through accomplishment."[3]

- Patience is necessary for mastery. One way to gain patience is to assume, at least for the time, that the task at hand is the only thing in the whole world there is to be done. Another way is to not worry about getting to your goal in the most efficient or direct manner. (If I worried about that, I would still be contemplating chapter 1 of this book!) Just get there any way you can. In retrospect, it will seem as if you did a lot of extra work. But that is not really true. No project that involves any degree of creativity is ever done in a straight line, free of confusion and blind alleys.
- If you can't do a lot, do a little. Set up secondary goals, instead of having just one overwhelming primary goal. Then concentrate on completing one secondary goal at a time.
- It might be useful to examine your resistance to "doing," to see if you can find a cause. Become clear about the cause, but don't use it

as an excuse for not carrying out the task. Often, the cause of resistance is either fear or conflicting motivations. If these are brought to light, one usually finds that they are not as much of a barrier as they seemed when they were subconscious.

- You need to be aware that inner and outer conditions can influence the perception of how well you are doing. I remember jogging once and finding it so hard to run at a certain pace, and I was thinking myself lazy. Then I realized that the road on which I was running was going uphill, when I had thought it was level—so the need for effort was real.
- If the task before you requires some creativity and you are stuck, just mess around with it; *play*. Don't stick strictly to a narrow goal. See what insights or enthusiasms you have that may be indirectly related to the stated goal.
- Don't expect perfection.
- Finally, don't get uptight when you fail, when your mastery is not up to the task at hand. We all fail often in our journey toward mastery. The trick is not to get discouraged, to keep at it.

> Ours is not a caravan of despair.
> Even though you have broken your vow a hundred times,
> come, come again.
>
> RUMI

The mastery of the self has a most important side effect, the development of self-confidence. This is an essential trait on the spiritual journey. You cannot rely entirely on others to get you where you want to go—although others, especially good teachers, can indeed help, and it is certainly more joyous to make the journey in the company of others. In the end, though, your progress depends a great deal on your own efforts (but you need to be careful about the ego slipping into the efforts), so you must have confidence in those efforts.

One reason progress depends on your own efforts is that the various stages of the journey become successively more subtle and require more strength. This means that you must develop that strength and be able to trust your own judgment and discernment. An aid in developing the necessary self-confidence is to recognize and appreciate what you *have* accomplished.

There are two cautions in learning mastery. The first is embodied in the saying, "What you master, masters you." Gaining self-confidence is fine, but don't let mastery inflate your sense of self. The second caution is to not fall into the trap of thinking you have mastery when you don't. Coleman Barks tells the following story:

> Nasrudin was standing with a rifle 50 yards from a wall. There were a number of small circles on the wall, and each had a bullet hole exactly in the middle.
>
> "Wonderful shooting," a friend said to Nasrudin. "How did you become such a good shot?"
>
> "It was quite simple," explained Nasrudin. "I shot first and then painted the circles."

MYSTICAL MASTERY

Mystical mastery concerns mastery of the Mind—mastery of your thought processes—and the ability to listen to your intuition (which comes from the djinn plane) throughout the day. Mystical mastery is much more rigorous than mastery in everyday life, for there is no respite, nowhere to hide. The world no longer divides into separate projects; there is just one goal, and all your energy and concentration are bent toward that goal.

Although mystical mastery sounds, and is, very difficult, it is not burdensome, because you want only that goal. There is no virtue in this mastery; it is simply that after a certain stage in your development, that is your willingly accepted task.

As a simple example of an intermediate stage in this mastery of the Mind, consider the fire breath of chapter 24—breathe in through the solar plexus, breathe out from the heart center, relaxing the heart area and radiating light in all directions. A mystic with some mastery would be able to do this for an hour without getting his or her attention caught up in a chain of thought, so there would be a virtually continuous awareness of the breath. This doesn't involve an iron control by the mystic; he or she would be quite relaxed, yet alert. Instead it involves practice in not getting one's awareness captured by the automatic processes of the Mind-brain—the associative process and emotional evaluation of thoughts.

Mystical mastery involves a thorough knowledge of the sources of energy within yourself—what turns you on, your bliss—and of the potential blockages of that energy. The mastery of the mystic—mastery of awareness and energy— gives true power, rather than just the appearance of power so common in our world. It is inevitably accompanied by gentleness and compassion.

A most interesting kind of power comes to those who have mastered their Minds. They are able to influence to some extent the direction of others' thoughts—not in an evil or manipulative way, and usually not in specific ways, such as willing someone to look at them, for example. But a true master, by concentrating in a certain way, would be able to make a group of people more calm and friendly, less agitated or angry. This is not done through the steely power of will; it happens simply because of the openness of the master's Mind, because he or she is not occupied with unnecessary thoughts of himself or herself. A master is also able, to some extent, to control the flow of events.

INSIGHT

If mastery is the ability to *do* what needs to be done, then insight is, at least in part, the ability to *see* what needs to be done. In relatively simple situations, insight is essentially synonymous with finding a simple organizational principle. As an example, in about 1600, Danish astronomer Tycho Brahe gave Johannes Kepler thousands of observations of the positions of planets in the sky. Kepler found that they all became simply organized if he assumed that the planets went around the sun in elliptical orbits. The organizational principle, the point of view that made all the data line up, was the principle of elliptical orbits.

ESSENCE & STRUCTURAL SIMILARITY

Most of the situations we encounter in everyday life are messier than Kepler's planetary orbit problem. There are typically myriad facts, most of which are inessential, and a few of which are essential for the insight at hand. Insight in these more complicated cases involves the ideas of structure and essence; we need to find a simple structure that summarizes the essence of the facts or perceptions. As an example, consider the following Nasrudin story:

> Someone saw Mulla Nasrudin searching for something on the ground.
> "What have you lost, Mulla?" he asked.
> "My key," said the Mulla.
> So they both went down on their knees and looked for it.
> After a time, the other man asked:
> "Where exactly did you drop it?"
> "In my own house."
> "Then why are we looking for it here?"
> "There is more light here than in my own house."[4]

The key stands for an understanding of oneself, the house for one's interior structure—psychological, djinn, angelic—and the ground outside the house for the external physical world, so full of attention-grabbing events (brightly lit). This short story has a structure that summarizes the essence of the many, many facts related to looking in the wrong place for what we really want.

This use of structural analogy or similarity to reveal essence is pervasive. A saying such as "Cutting off your nose to spite your face" can summarize someone's self-destructive behavior. Metaphors, similes, analogies, myth, poetry, music, and much of good literature all make use of structural similarity. The search for essence is the driving force for the highest levels of physics where the physicists look for a single mathematical law to summarize the behavior of all matter. The mystic, carrying the idea of essence to its farthest reaches, seeks the simple structure behind the myriad facts of all of existence.

DEVELOPING INSIGHT

Most people are more aware of the need to develop mastery than they are of the need to develop insight, but insight is important in directing our efforts so here are a few suggestions that might help to develop it.

- The first step is to simply become aware of the need to develop insight. When you do this—for any attribute, not just insight—your Mind has its own way of developing that attribute. You become what you concentrate on. You become attuned to a certain set of the thought-forms of the djinn plane and even the forms of the angelic plane.

- You can train your mind to look for simple structure (such as Kepler's ellipses) and congruence of structure (analogies). Some conventional education, particularly in-depth teaching of language or literature, is good at this. The course of studies in the Pythagorean mystery (mystical) schools, where all students had to learn geometry, was designed in part to teach these ideas.

- One way to obtain insight into a problem or situation is to concentrate on it for a while and then periodically release the concentration. Reverie and even sleep can help. It often happens that ideas occur in the release period. The reason is that we usually make implicit, overly restrictive assumptions when we concentrate, but release these assumptions when we relax. We are also more likely to get in touch with the djinn plane, the plane of ideas, during relaxation.

- It helps to become aware of the need for clarity in your thought. We usually stop short of sufficient clarity. Keep at it; clarity is paid back a hundredfold. It makes each step more secure as a foundation for the next insight and makes each insight sharper, more accurate, and more satisfying.

- For insights into the mystical path, including insights into blockages and inaccurate, restrictive points of view, I recommend the teaching tales of Idries Shah.[5] These are often childlike and humorous. They use simple stories that illustrate structures on the djinn and angelic planes, as well as in human nature.

DEPTH OF INSIGHT & TIME

Insight into the nature of existence takes time to develop. At each stage of our lives, we have a perspective that can support only a certain range of insights. Some insights are far outside our point of view, so that when we are presented with them, there is little overlap or meshing between the new insight and the current structure. For example, I might tell you that you had some say in choosing your parents. This would seem totally ridiculous if you knew nothing of the djinn plane or that there was life before birth—and even if you did know that, it might still seem ridiculous until your "knowing" had matured. When the insights are far outside your current perspective, you perceive them as either irrelevant or false. (This is the explanation of the mystical saying, "The secret protects itself.") Your mind must be ready to accept an insight before its presentation can help you.

(If you are willing to consider this "choice" idea, there are additional points you should be aware of. Our djinn being was very naive, in an earthly sense, when making the choice. So if your choice of parents seems less than optimal, it does not reflect upon your judgment. Also, rest assured that you did not choose troublesome parents to give you problems to work through.)

After you have reached the point where you can accept an insight of a certain level, you must integrate it into your whole system of thought before you are ready for the next level. Deeper and deeper insights must therefore be presented in stages. All this takes time. This part of mystical training, the acceptance and integration of deep insights, cannot be hurried. As Evans-Wentz, the translator of Tibetan Buddhist monk Padmasambhava's work says, "An acorn is not an oak."[6]

WISDOM

Wisdom certainly involves insight, but it involves other skills as well: a fine sense of judgment; and the ability to keep your personal biases from distorting your judgment.

Wisdom also gives a perspective on insight. The point is not just to see the structure of existence, but also to see and experience the mystery of existence. "The eye goes blind when it only wants to see why," says Rumi.

BEAUTY

The practice of each of the attributes—mastery, insight, and beauty—corresponds to a possible path, a way of getting to what is really desired. Of these, the creation and appreciation of beauty is most closely related to our innermost desire. Mastery and insight are more concerned with the structure of existence (jnana), while beauty is more concerned with the emotional feel or experience of existence (bhakti). We can *master* the forms of existence or we can stand outside and insightfully *perceive* existence, but the perception of beauty invokes *an appreciation* of existence as well as *a longing* for what the beauty implies. Beauty reminds us of what could be and of what has been. Beauty is cutting, poignant. It partly hides and partly reveals. It melts you and at the same time energizes you. At its most powerful, it lays you bare and shatters your conceptual framework.

Beauty takes many forms: natural scenes, the human form, visual art, music, mathematical and linguistic elegance, and internal vision. What makes something beautiful? This, of course, is an age-old question to which there is no definitive answer. But I believe that part of the answer is related to the higher planes. Something is beautiful here insofar as it evokes the beauty of the djinn and angelic planes.

Why is there beauty on the higher planes? Because beauty is spirit with form, and since the higher planes are closer to the origin of existence than our world here is, they embody more spirit. Also, we dimly remember those planes from our long stay there before we were born on the physical plane. Because of this, beauty sometimes makes us feel as if we are "coming home."

BEAUTY AS A PATH

How is beauty to be used as a path? There are two ways. One involves having the outlook of the idealized artist, always trying to create beauty—to create physical forms or intellectual constructs that resonate with forms on the djinn or angelic planes.

An artist starts wherever his or her mastery, insight, and sense of beauty are. In the struggle to create artistic beauty and insight, an artist's mode of expression does not stay static. If this evolution of expression is honestly pursued through all its levels—that is, if the artist's energy and ideals hold up, and the temptation to produce art strictly for money or acclaim is avoided—it brings her or him ever closer to the goals of existence, the creative response to the original longing.

The other aspect of beauty as a path is purely bhakti—a total devotion to the beauty of { } and the highest parts of the djinn and angelic planes. Beauty and this longing are closely intertwined on this path.

INNER BEAUTY

Finally, there is one more aspect of beauty on the mystical path. As you progress on the mystical journey, your own being becomes more beautiful. If you purify and purify and purify yourself, so that you do not dwell on irrelevant details and the negative, and distill and distill and distill your essence, until you are in intimate contact with the djinn and angelic planes, and { }, then others will perceive you as being beautiful (and powerful!). There is a harmony between inner and outer in this beauty. It is not a goal that can be achieved directly, by cosmetic means; it is a byproduct of your mystical progress.

VIRTUE

An idea related to attributes is that of virtue. A sampling of virtues would include patience, a concern for the welfare of others (compassion), mastery, humility, sexual mores, being responsible, talking an appropriate amount, truthfulness, moderation, respect, even performing one's spiritual practices.

Virtues are necessary to a mystic's development. (Hazrat Inayat Khan's wonderful book, *Creating the Person* includes twenty-three two-page essays on the virtues a mystic might wish to develop.) Virtues are important because there is a natural law whose consequence is that you cannot progress far along the spiritual path if you don't practice these virtues. This is not a stern or vindictive law set up by a judgmental God; instead it is a law that derives from the unavoidably limiting perspective of a person who concentrates on herself or himself, a perspective that prevents the perception of the higher, more beautiful realms of the djinn and angelic planes.

If you are not truthful with others, for example, it is impossible to be truthful with yourself; and if you are not truthful with yourself, you will never be able to discern the true nature of your being. If you don't practice moderation to a sufficient degree, it will be difficult to acquire a balanced mastery. If your sexual mores are outside certain bounds, it implies you don't have proper respect for others, or yourself. This, in turn, implies that your lesser self is preventing your greater self from realizing its potential.

Because of this natural law, it is necessary for the teacher of a prospective mystic to facilitate the development of these virtues in his or her students. This is a significant part of mystical training. These virtues are a *sine qua non* for spiritual development past a certain point.

Virtues, when viewed in this way, are seen as a means of progressing toward the goal, but there are two other, less healthy ways of viewing them. First, you can think of your practice of virtues as a yardstick or measure of your spiritual progress. The yardstick perspective is correct in one sense, because virtues develop automatically when you progress properly on the path. But if, for example, you consistently use your compassion as a spiritual gauge, chances are that the practice of compassion will not advance you toward the goal. The practice of compassion *can* be a valid way of progressing for some, because it relaxes the strong focus on the lower self. But if you practice compassion with the thought that it is a yardstick or indicator—rather than a means, or simply because it comes naturally to you—it will not carry you far along the path.

The other less healthy way of viewing virtues is practicing them because you are trying to please an authority—parents, teachers, society at large, scripture, or your concept of God. This point of view is valid up to a certain point, but if, after a certain stage in your spiritual development, you don't understand or feel for yourself why a virtue is beneficial, that virtue will not be practiced in a balanced, appropriate way, and the virtue will no longer engender further progress. At some point, you must drop the idea that you are gaining merit—earning good marks from an outside authority—by practicing virtues. There is ultimately no gain of merit; there is only progress on the journey.

GOOD & BAD

Virtue, in its pleasing-an-authority guise, is often associated with good and bad. The good-bad dichotomy is not useful on the mystical journey. We could, perhaps, speak of good and missed opportunities, but good-bad superimposes a false and therefore misleading structure on one's actions. "Bad" introduces an unnecessary tension, a tension that chokes off joyous perception of the other realms. It treats human beings the same as Pavlov's conditioned dogs.

THE GREAT SECRET

God was so full of wine last night,
So full of wine That He let a great secret slip.

He said:
There is no one on this earth
Who needs a pardon from Me—
For there is really no such thing,
No such thing
As sin!

HAFIZ

27

RETREATS, TEACHERS

The aim of practices is to enable your Mind to bring the higher planes into awareness, to communicate with the Great Beings who dwell on those planes, and to go as far as you can toward the goals of existence. To do this, you must change the habitual behavior of the Mind-brain. If you find that daily practices do not bring about changes in awareness as rapidly as you would wish, you might consider a retreat.

RETREATS

The idea behind a spiritual retreat is that if you can keep your Mind-brain out of its habitual ruts for three days or more, you can begin to change its deeper structure. By not feeding energy into the maintenance of your habitual, constricted view of the world, you can increase the quality and depth of your awareness. A retreat can also help familiarize you with how it feels to be aware on the higher planes. Some people find that the concentrated form of practice associated with a retreat is essential for their progress.

TYPES OF RETREATS

There are many types of retreats. It is useful to classify them according to four criteria. The first criterion is the amount of contact with other retreatants; the retreat can be an individual retreat, a retreat done entirely as a group, or something in between.

The second criterion is the stature of the retreat guide. It is best if she or he has a good deal of mystical insight, although this is a very difficult quality to judge, and a fair amount of experience guiding retreats. The retreat guide sets the tone—bhakti, jnana, psychological—and the style of practice. A highly skilled guide, especially in less group-oriented retreats, will vary the tone, style, and level to suit the student.

The third criterion is the amount of lecture or information time versus the amount of practice time, and the fourth is the severity of the practices, from gentle to rigorous. The latter two variables will also fall under the aegis of the guide.

My recommendation is to begin with a retreat that is not too severe, a group retreat where one is on silence only part of the day, for example. There are two reasons for this preference. The first reason is that we draw inspiration from other retreatants. When we are struggling, their presence can help. In addition, as a retreat progresses and the participants drop their masks and become more open, we are able to see a true beauty, majesty, and power in them, qualities we would not see in other circumstances. This can contribute greatly to the retreat, as well as to our life beyond the retreat.

The second reason has to do with strength. A retreat can be a time of somewhat painful changes of mental habits. If you take an individual retreat, seeing only your guide, and him or her for only a few minutes a day, the negative aspects of change can be overwhelming. Unless you are emotionally and mentally strong, you can feel as if you have lost the basis of your personality, that your guidelines have snapped. The relatively balanced schedule and the presence of the group helps moderate these effects. I am not saying, of course, that a rigorous retreat will necessarily be a psychologically undermining experience. In my opinion, though, it is better to have some group retreat experience under your belt before trying an individual retreat.

EFFECT OF RETREATS

Suppose that, for the most part, you can keep your Mind from dwelling on its usual thoughts for, say, a two-day retreat. Even in that short time, there will be a certain level of habitual thinking that has not been fed energy and will therefore begin to lose its influence on you. That is, there will be a certain set of below-the-level-of-consciousness microemotions, those mechanistic guides of thought-chains, that you have dropped or at least weakened. If you can comfortably go four days, the level of habitual thoughts that have been weakened will be even deeper.

Getting rid of those mechanistic thought-guides is very freeing. After the retreat, you will probably notice it as a clarity of mind and perhaps as an irritation toward those circumstances that throw you back into the old habits.

THE TEACHER

In the West, the religious teacher typically has, in addition to a certain social role, approximately the same role as a good teacher of any subject. In the East and Middle East, however, a real teacher is a mystic. (There are, of course, valid mystical teachers in the West also and many teachers in the East and Middle East who are not mystics.) He or she can see your inner condition—your potentially great qualities and what blocks you from developing these qualities. Because of this ability to perceive, and his or her inner power, the mystic-teacher can help you achieve what is possible for you. It is essential that you find a good teacher if you really want to progress past a certain point on the mystical path.

The problem is how to find and recognize a good teacher. Because spiritual evolution leads us to develop our own unique gifts, mystical teachers have a wide range of personality traits. Many teachers, at least outwardly, do not have an aura of holiness or spirituality about them. There are, however, a few characteristics they commonly share. They are usually courteous. They usually have great patience and do not become frustrated easily. They have a clear attention and are almost never careless with their Minds. Existence is vibrant for them. Sometimes they seem not to observe the normal rules of social exchange because they no longer engage in the psychological games most people play (or they wish to counter the games you are playing).

There are many classic descriptions of mystical teachers, often diluted by hyperbole and mythologizing. I have chosen two that I believe are not inflated:

> He has keen fiery insight and vast dignity
> like the night sky.
>
> RUMI

> They were careful.
> as someone crossing an iced-over stream.
> Alert as a warrior in enemy territory.
> Courteous as a guest.
> Fluid as melting ice.
> Shapable as a block of wood.
> Receptive as a valley.
> Clear as a glass of water.
>
> LAO-TZU

A few words of caution about choosing a teacher. First, you might be tempted to judge a potential teacher by how psychically gifted she or he is—by this I mean the ability to see auras, read minds, or produce miraculous physical effects or psychological states. This is often not a good gauge. A true teacher will seldom publicly display his or her abilities in this area. Second, a mystic, even a good one, has not given up all self-oriented behavior. (Think of yourself becoming a teacher in ten years. Can you imagine yourself being anywhere near perfect?) So don't expect a perfect human being. Third, a good teacher will not undermine your autonomy.

If you have decided to seriously explore mysticism, the most fruitful way of proceeding is to find a good teacher and stay with him or her over a period of years. There are many levels that a teacher must guide you through, by giving you practices and presenting new points of view on existence for you to think about and absorb. One of the functions of a teacher is to be a cheerleader; the teacher can point out to you your good, albeit perhaps hidden, qualities. This is helpful because much of our obscuration is due to a lack of true self-confidence, and the teacher needs to instill that confidence.

Finally, there is a tendency in the West to go to seminars conducted by teachers from many different traditions. You may enjoy shopping around for a while. Seminars and books can sustain you at the beginning of your quest, but you should try to find and settle down with a good teacher as soon as you comfortably can.

28

THE PHYSICAL PLANE, BRAIN FUNCTIONS & MYSTICAL PRACTICES

Know that the body nurtures the spirit, helps it grow, and then gives it the wrong advice.

RUMI

To understand the goals and methodology of mystical practices, it is best to start with the pluses and minuses of the physical plane.

HOW THE BODY HELPS US GROW

How do the physical brain-body and the physical universe nurture the spirit and help it grow?

- The brain is an exquisite instrument for helping the Mind fulfill the goals of its existence.

- The physical plane is concrete, so existence here is less confusing than it is on the other planes. Because of this, we can more easily learn how to focus our attention here.
- The concreteness of the physical plane and the ability to focus our attention give us an opportunity to gain mastery of our selves, a mastery that is difficult to attain on the other planes.
- Reason is more easily learned on the physical plane, as is the balance between reason and creative imagination. Because of this, clarity of intelligence and wisdom are also more easily gained here.
- We can learn here to notice, appreciate, and create beauty.
- We can more easily work on developing many of the qualities or attributes here than we can on the other planes.
- There are many unique opportunities on the physical plane for creativity and friendship-intimacy.
- Finally, because of the understanding we can gain here, existence on the physical plane allows us to take fuller advantage of the possibilities on the djinn and angelic planes.

WRONG ADVICE GIVEN BY THE BODY

- The physical brain-body gives the Mind the impression that *physical* existence is all there is to existence. This delusion arises because, in the struggle to grow up and exist in the physical world, the Mind has had to concentrate all its attention on the physical plane. (The delusion is made even more convincing by the materialistic orientation of our society.)
- The body gives the Mind an exaggerated view of the Mind's limitations, because the Mind comes to believe that its familiar surroundings—perceptual and conceptual—constitute all of existence.
- It is absolutely essential that the aspiring mystic understand the emotional entanglement of the brain and the Mind. To see this perspective,

first think of the body as simply an extraordinarily sophisticated mechanism (à la the materialists) with no associated Mind. It has neural circuitry that specializes in emotions and is the basis for the likes and dislikes that are unique to each of us.

Now enter the Mind. When it first associates with the body, the task of learning how to operate that mechanism is enormous; it absorbs all the Mind's attention. During that period of intense concentration on the body, the Mind comes to think of the body's emotions as its own emotions. It thinks that all our daily desires, preferences, goals, and discomforts are its own, whereas 98 percent of them originate in the brain-body. Thus we fall into the trap of letting our body impose its emotions and "choices" on our Mind; the puppeteer has become the slave of the puppet. (A good example of this slavery is our inability to stop the brain's chatter. The problem is not really that our brain chatters, but that our Mind listens to it.)

Therefore, to gain our true freedom, to open up to the vastness of existence, to reduce our fear of death, our Mind must throw off its slavery to the brain-based emotions and preferences that, second by second, guide our actions and thoughts. That is the goal of many of the practices of part 5.

- The overall perspective or mindset that we learn during our physical existence stays with us after death. If that perspective is restrictive, and usually it is, we are limited in our experiences of the nonphysical planes after death. Most mindsets, of course, also severely limit us during our life here.

WRONG ADVICE & BRAIN FUNCTIONS

The different functions of the brain participate in giving us wrong advice in different ways:

PERCEPTION

The Mind forms the habit of believing that the only perception is physical perception. It learns—partly through societal pressure—to ignore intuitive perception, and thus loses the faculty of perceiving on the other planes. This loss means we cannot appreciate others as deeply as possible because we do not see the other's whole self.

AWARENESS

The Mind comes to focus its awareness exclusively on the goings-on of its individual brain. It forgets there is a vast expanse of nonphysical existence outside the brain. It does not remember that individual existences are not as separate on the other planes as they appear to be here.

MEMORY

Not only does the Mind limit its awareness to the physical plane, it limits itself even further by giving too much importance to the memory categories of the brain. As we grow older, the Mind comes to believe that anything outside these categories is not worth its attention.

CONCEPTS

Even more than our collection of factual memories, our collection of concepts about the structure of existence limits us. Through laziness (or perhaps through a premature confidence in ourselves), the collection becomes sacrosanct and static; there is no room for growth.

ASSOCIATION, CHAINS OF THOUGHT

The brain has a mechanism whereby it associates one thought with another. This gives rise to chains of thought. The Mind falls into the habit of not exercising its freedom of choice, so these chains of thought often continue mechanistically, as if we had little freedom to choose our thoughts.

EMOTIONS

The Mind falls into the habit of believing that the only emotions are the ones that register strongly in the brain (have a strong neural correlate), but there are many emotions that are more closely associated with the nonphysical planes. If we pay attention only to brain-based emotions, then these higher emotions, and the motivations and goals associated with them, are ignored in favor of lower emotions and goals.

MICROEMOTIONS

The Mind, in conjunction with the brain's mechanisms, learns to respond to a restricted set of preferences. These get built into the brain's circuitry and mechanistically dictate the flow of thought.

MYSTICAL PRACTICES

The goals of mystical practices are: to relax the strong focus of your Mind on what is happening in the brain; to alter your overall mindset, your view of what reality is like, what is possible and not possible, and what your potential is; to find ways of enhancing your perception on the other planes; to become attuned to and guided by higher emotions; to commune with the Great Beings and {}; and to develop the qualities of yourself until you become a Great Being, capable of enhancing the quality of all existence. With these goals and the limiting properties of the brain in mind, I will comment on the various practices.

WATCHING YOUR THOUGHTS

When you watch your thoughts, there are three results:

1. You see (much to your initial chagrin and frustration) how mechanistic your thoughts are and how little control you have over them.

2. You begin to get the idea, experientially, that there is something in you deeper than your brain thoughts.

3. The energy that feeds the mechanistic chains of thoughts comes from focusing your attention on the content and emotional import of these chains. If you focus instead on observing the thoughts, rather than getting caught up in the ensnaring emotions of the content, that energy dies down after a while, leaving room for the Mind to begin to be aware on the nonphysical planes.

WATCHING THE BREATH, CHANTING

If you can focus on your breath or a chant for, say, half an hour, you lessen the focus of your Mind on your mechanistic, associative, microemotion-driven thoughts. This helps you break the habit of always focusing on your brain thoughts.

It takes a certain amount and type of energy for your Mind to focus on your mechanistic thoughts. Focusing on your breath or a chant redirects that energy, often more effectively than watching your thoughts—freeing your Mind and making it more open to experience on the nonphysical planes.

The breath or chant reminds your Mind, in a nonconceptual, metaphorical way of the nature of the nonphysical planes. This helps your Mind relearn how to perceive on these planes. The breath also reminds the Mind of the highest emotions, and of { }, the source and goal of existence.

RETREATS

A retreat provides a longer time during which your Mind is not focusing its awareness on your habitual guiding microemotions and mindsets. This diminishes the influence of microemotions and restrictive mindsets. You literally think differently after a retreat; the neural circuitry has been altered by your not thinking in the same old ruts.

PRACTICES IN LIFE

The habits of the Mind—thinking the physical world is all there is, experiencing fear, anger, and self-pity—are strengthened by our daily use of them. One effective way to disrupt and weaken these habits is to perform practices such as watching the breath during everyday life. In fact, this type of practice is essential past a certain point because there is no other way to replace these narrow habitual points of view with a broader perspective.

You can cease to be the captive of your neurochemically related emotions and moods by becoming aware of them and realizing they need not dictate your actions and thoughts.

You can alter your mindset, and thus your self, by becoming more attuned to where your awareness is throughout the day. Then you can see how to change the focus and quality of your moment-to-moment awareness, so that, step by small step, you gain true mastery and compassionate power, true majesty and beauty, true wisdom.

THE PRACTICE OF THE PRESENCE OF GOD

At a somewhat more advanced stage in your spiritual development, you may be able to seek the presence of { } during much of the day. This opens you to the most exalted realms of the higher planes.

THE ART OF THE SELF

ELIMINATING RESTRICTIVE MINDSETS

During the course of your life here, you usually acquire a restrictive mindset, a narrow focus of the Mind, a narrow perspective. One way to expand that perspective is to choose one of your major restrictive mindsets—say anger or self-pity—and actively refuse to let it influence you for one hour a day.

By observation, you need to become aware of what your motivations are, and what the motivations behind those motivations are, until you come to the highest motivations of all. You can also observe this in others but do not be judgmental, either of others or yourself.

It is a boon to your self if you concentrate on certain qualities—insight, compassion, mastery, beauty—in such a way that they become part of you. You should aim to acquire something of the qualities that characterize the Great Beings.

Along with all these practices, it is good if you can be at ease with your-self, accepting that, as a finite being, you will never become perfect. It is also good if you can appreciate the beauty and subtlety of Nature and the qualities of others.

Finally, because human beings are not as separate from one another as we appear on the physical plane, we need to be aware of and promote harmony in our interactions with others.

THE MYSTIC & SOCIETY

As a mystic progresses, what are his or her goals? The underlying goals are friendship, intimacy, and creativity. But how do they play out in the life of a mystic? There is wide variation here. The primary concern of some mystics is insight into, and the experiential knowing of, the nature of existence—intimacy with existence. For others, it is knowing the Great Beings who have their existence on the djinn and angelic planes. The mystics who are absorbed by these goals often live in isolation, in caves in the Himalayas, or in monasteries. Those who do so live outside the cycle of change; they do not participate in the potential inherent in human society.[1]

The mystics I am concerned with do participate in society. These mystics are not just focused on their own enlightenment; that feels to them like too narrow an aim. Instead, they are also vitally concerned with interpersonal interactions here on earth. I will first describe the mystic's perspective on society in the larger sense, and then come back to friendship, which is the natural societal focus of most mystics.

THE MYSTICAL SOCIETY OF THE FUTURE

What is the potential for society in a mystical sense? It is difficult to comprehend. Think of your highest moments of friendship, intimacy, and creativity, and imagine what life would be like if everyone were in that state—and even higher states—much of the time. The friction, the negativity, and the fear of our society would fall away and be replaced by the joy of existence. There would still be sadness, but it would not unduly weigh us down. Mysticism would not be a belief; it would simply be the milieu in which we lived. Its practice would not be separate from ordinary life, as religious practice often is now. Such a society is wonderful to contemplate, but we cannot expect it for the majority of humanity for many thousands of years.

SOCIETY TODAY

Humanity has progressed materially over the past twenty-five hundred years. Physical science has advanced and aided material progress. Society has progressed educationally, with many more people now having access to the wisdom of civilization. Individualism in the West has brought a welcome degree of freedom.

But the present world is far from reaching its potential: Progress is distributed unevenly; personal freedom is often used to satisfy lower, self-centered desires that are distortions of the goal of existence; the planet's ecology is being severely damaged; and there is a rapid global drift toward the dead end of materialism, which engenders a dissatisfaction with life because it mistakes a small, lower goal for the ultimate aim.

Physical science, because of its support of materialism, its criticism of mysticism, and its seductive seeming-certainty, has the potential to impede society's progress just as religion has occasionally done in the past (and still does in some instances in the present). A paradigm serves a purpose for a period, but then lingers and outlives its usefulness. Physical science will continue to be useful in many senses in the foreseeable future, of course, but its materialistic thrust should not determine the way in which humanity views the cosmos.

What is the future of our Western materialistic society? Current trends suggest that the overly consumption-oriented lifestyle of the West will not last long (unless there is a major breakthrough in solar energy). My guess is that it will end, either through disaster[2]—An energy crisis? The needs of less developed countries? Famine? Terrorists?—or economic pressures within sixty years, and probably sooner.

(There are people of goodwill whose actions *do* have the proper orientation even though they have no overt leanings toward mysticism. But they do not have the in-depth wisdom that a mystic has.)

As long as only a small percentage of people seriously explore mysticism, society will languish. That *must* be because without mysticism a person's actions do not have the proper orientation. But if, say, 5 percent of the population were to have a mystic's orientation, then there would be many possibilities that are not open now.

POTENTIAL IMPROVEMENTS IN SOCIETY

How would the mystic improve our society? I have a few suggestions, although I don't know how they could be carried out. First, general governmental policy is currently driven in large part by economic considerations, in which human beings are viewed primarily as economic entities. That should change. The quality of the environment and the benefits of more natural surroundings should be emphasized even more than it is now. The workplace

should be more a place of creativity and camaraderie, rather than one of boredom, resentment at the work and long hours, and fear for one's job.

Perhaps most important, education needs to be rethought. The "rhythm"
of many schools (as well as the rhythm of society in general) should be slowed
down. The inculcation of the competitive mode should be moderated. Both
mastery and insight need to be better taught. Even more than these, we need
to teach students about their own profound nature as well as a deep respect
for others.

What is the role of mystics in these changes? One possibility is for them to
become involved in government, business, and education and try to make
changes just as other citizens do—and mystics do indeed do that. There are,
however, other ways that the mystic participates in society. He or she is aware
of the need to establish a healthy view on religion—actually, not on religion,
but on the true nature of existence. He or she is aware of the potential in individual and group interactions. And he or she, if very powerful and wise, can
help to change the goals of our current human civilization.

LOVE & FRIENDSHIP

I have avoided using the word *love* in this book because the current usage di-
lutes its true meaning. Instead, I have used *friendship*. Friendship is an appreciation of the other as a miniature of the cosmos, as a potentially, and perhaps
actually, magnificent Being, as a window on all of existence. Your intimate
friend is a source of enthusiasm, humor, insight, comfort; someone who wishes
to know you and to be known by you. Of all the forms on the physical plane,
friendship comes the closest to satisfying the original longing. It banishes
loneliness. It creates intimacy. There is unlimited possibility for creativity
within friendship, both in the inspiration and encouragement each gives the
other to create individually, and more directly in the interactions between
friends. Rumi captures something of friendship and intimacy in this poem:

A mouse and a frog meet every morning
on the riverbank.
They sit in a nook of the ground and talk.

Each morning, the second they see each other,
they open easily, telling stories and dreams and secrets,
empty of any fear or suspicious holding-back.

To watch and listen to these two
is to understand how, as it's written,
sometimes when two beings come together,
Christ becomes visible.

The mouse starts laughing out a story he hasn't thought of
in five years, and the telling might take five years!
There's no blocking the speechflow-river-running-
all-carrying momentum
that true intimacy is. . . .

Friend sits by Friend, and the tablets appear,
They read the mysteries
off each other's foreheads.

So the mystic seeks friendship and seeks to encourage friendship. And not just in pairs; a group of friends, each with clear sight and joyous energy, is a treasure far beyond gold. The following story by Idries Shah gives a glimpse of the wild, joyous energy generated by a group of mystics. It also implies that each of us has his or her own gifts, gifts that most readily emerge in the company of mystics (called "demons" in the story).

THE MAN WITH THE WEN

Once long ago, in old Japan, there was a man who spent his days trudging up and down the mountains collecting wood. This he used to burn, and to make charcoal, for he was unable to make a living in any other way. This unfortunate fellow thought that the gods were in some way displeased with him, for he had on his left cheek a large and disfiguring swelling: what people call a wen.

He had gone to many doctors, but whatever treatment they had prescribed had never been of any use. He was so distressed at his appearance that he shunned other people and gradually became more and more miserable. His wife tried to be cheerful about the matter and pretended to be unaware of it; however, in the end it made her hate him.

One day the charcoal burner went slowly up the mountain track, fingering his wen with exploring fingers, positive that it was larger than the day before. Suddenly, the thunder rolled and heavy rain began to fall.

"O Merciful Heaven," he cried, "so far from home and so little wood, and now this downpour. Where can I shelter?"

He took refuge in a hollow tree. But just as quickly as the storm had begun, it ceased. The charcoal burner fingered his wen, and was just about to creep out of the tree when he heard the tramp of feet. The rays of the setting sun played on a group of people who came marching along the mountain path, lighting them with a crimson glow.

"Whoever can they be?" wondered the man. He still remained inside the hollow tree, for the sound of wild piping came to his ears. With staring eyes he gazed at a multitude of creatures; they were the strangest he had ever seen in his life. There must have been about a hundred of them, a troop of what he now realized were some sort of enchanted beings. They were all of strange shapes and sizes.

Not daring to show himself, the frightened charcoal burner peeped through a knothole and held his breath. They came to a stop just near his hiding place, and the stamping and music grew louder. They made a large circle, ambling or hopping, round and round, with the head demon in the middle. They lit a huge bonfire and danced round it, shouting and singing at the top of their voices.

The firelight gleamed on furry legs, shining tusks, and flashing eyes. As he watched and heard the music, the charcoal burner became as gay as they. Forgotten was his wen and his predicament; he leaped into the firelight and his feet carried him round in a most lively dance. His wen bobbed about, but he did not even try to cover it as usual with one hand. His arms were flung into the air, and he danced crazily, willing, and fey, with all the others, enjoying themselves round the fire.

"Well done! Excellent timing!" shouted the head demon, "Keep it up, human being, we are much entertained!" Each demon roared or screeched encouragement. The man danced like one whose very life depended on his feet not touching the ground for more than a split second.

At last, completely worn out, he came to a sudden stop. "You have danced well," said the head demon. "We have been immensely privileged to have you in our little company. Never have we seen a human who could keep up with our ideas of revelry, let alone surpass us!"

"No, no," said the charcoal burner politely, "It was most remarkably good of you to allow my faltering steps to . . . "

"Faltering steps!" You are a master of the dance!" roared the head demon. "I speak for all of my people when I say we have tonight, in fact, learned much in the way of steps from you! Perhaps we can keep your wen to remember you by." And with just a prick, the wen—and the troop of dancers—vanished.

The man went home to his wife, whose love returned, as strong and beautiful as it had been on their wedding day. And they found a hundred silver coins in the bottom of his basket.[3]

MYSTICAL "RELIGION"

Every mystic who chooses to participate in society acts as a teacher, a spiritual guide to those seeking to know the cosmos—even if the mystic does not formally have students. Teaching styles of mystics vary greatly, but we can abstract a general framework for the teaching, a framework that holds no matter what the background or methodology of the mystic. The tenets of this universal mystical religion, which is somewhat different from the religions familiar to most of us, are as follows:[4]

- It is both democratic and hierarchical; all are given respect, but there are those who know and see and experience much more than the average person and are therefore capable of being teachers.

- It is transmitted from teacher to student; it is not possible to reach high levels on your own. Typically, a group of students will gather around a teacher, who will teach them intensively. This orientation around mystics of true accomplishment implies there is little centralized administrative authority, although there will be cooperation and friendship among groups.

- It is the religion of experience—not just the reading, reasoning, and repetition that is a part of many religions, but true experience: the experience, before you die, of what awareness is like after you die; or the experience of knowing Great Beings on the djinn or angelic plane. The teacher shows the student how to gain access to this experience. There would be little dogma and no Bible as absolute authority, but there would be a wealth of poetic, insightful writing that the student may wish to use for guidance.

- Practitioners of this religion are tolerant of practitioners of all sincere religions, for it is wonderful and comforting to have companions on the path. And yet true mysticism, even though broadly tolerant, is a narrow path, based on an accurate understanding of the reason for and nature of existence.

- There is no strict applies-to-all code of conduct—about diet, dress, drinking, or pacifism, for example (although the student, and of course the teacher, is expected to be respectful of others). Such a code of conduct, especially at more advanced levels, would run counter to the goal of developing truly magnificent wise beings who are powerfully self-sufficient, compassionate, and capable of deep friendship.
- Teaching and advice for students is certainly available, but there is no compulsion toward a particular belief in this mystical religion, for compulsion does not lead to a proper appreciation of the truth.
- The practices and outer forms of mystical religion will constantly change. The reason is that in each time and place, there is a mindset that severely limits the worldview of all those who are not mystics. Therefore, the practices and outer forms of mystical religions must be tailored toward dissolving the blockages specific to the times. Even within a group of students, what they need at one stage (long periods of meditation and retreat, for example) will be different from what they need at another stage (revelry, so they can appreciate the joy of life). In fact, this dynamic, rather than static, stance is a keynote of mystics.

> If a gnostic seeker of knowledge is really a gnostic,
> he or she cannot stay tied to one form of belief.
>
> IBN ARABI, *KERNEL OF THE KERNEL*

- Finally, the religion of the mystic is natural. Mysticism and everyday life are not to be separated. The mystic's domain is the nature of existence, all of existence, so how could mysticism not be natural?

It would be good indeed if this mystical religion and society were not so far apart, but that is not true now. At this point, even segments of some religions, in addition to science and other institutions of society, are antithetical to mysticism.

Those on the way are almost invisible
to those who are not. A man or a woman
recognizes God and starts out. The others
say he or she is losing faith.

RUMI

PROGRAMMING THE UNIVERSE

There is one more role for the mystic in society. The mystic often operates in
relatively small groups here on earth. Because of their deep, conscious connection to the higher djinn and angelic planes, however, they have leverage on the
events of the physical plane. This ability to affect what happens on earth by
operating in the djinn or angelic plane has been called participating in the
programming of the universe.[5]

To explain this participation, I will give an example. As background, recall
that I stressed in chapter 3 that there is not a detailed, fixed blueprint for the
cosmos; a nonspontaneous universe is pointless for { }. There are, nevertheless, plans of varying degrees of scope, some small and some large. These
plans are not devised by { }, however (except for an overall, general, nonspe-
cific plan), but rather by the beings of existence. To illustrate how powerful
beings can participate in this planning, I will make up a story (although it is
not concocted out of whole cloth) about Pythagoras, the Greek mathematician
and mystic.

Pythagoras, who died about 500 B.C., lived after the flowering and decline
of the Egyptian empire. The Egyptians were excellent mystics in the sense that
they knew a good deal about the djinn plane, especially the magical parts.
Through the Egyptian mystery schools, Pythagoras was heir to their knowledge, but he could see that the Egyptian line of mysticism had played itself
out; there were no significant possibilities left for creativity and especially for
friendship-intimacy.

Pythagoras could also see, with his powerful mystical insight, that two steps were needed in order to create the potential for further steps along the mystical path. The first was that humanity had to come to a more accurate understanding of the nature—the *mathematical* nature—of the physical universe, so that certain technological and societal advances could come about. And the second was that a new, more thorough and pervasive form of education was needed. He gave explicit form to these in his lifetime by stressing geometry and by founding a school.

He also did something else. Because he was a mystic of enormous power and insight, he could cause things to happen on the djinn plane. What he did was reset the zeitgeist; that is, he reset the general djinn thought-forms that circumscribe human thought. Whereas before Pythagoras, the zeitgeist was magiclike and less oriented toward individuals, after Pythagoras, it was more akin to analytic thought and more individual-oriented.

Such resettings don't have their complete effect immediately; they take time. And it is only now, twenty-five hundred years later, that we see the fruit of what Pythagoras set in motion. With the culmination of the Pythagorean cycle, we are now ready for a new zeitgeist, one less analytical, less materialistic, more oriented toward relations between beings. Like love stories, but not exactly.

LOCALIZATION

Localization is one of the primary pieces of evidence cited in favor of the existence of particles. I will give an example of localization and then explain why it does not provide convincing evidence that particles exist.

ELECTRON-FILM EXAMPLE

The localization effect is best explained by an example. Suppose we shoot an electron (or more precisely, an electron wave function) at a piece of film that is made up of many small grains of a silver compound that is chemically activated when an electron wave function hits it. Assume that the wave function is spread out over many grains, as in figure A.1 (where "many" equals 4).

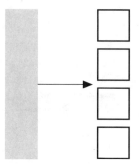

FIGURE A.1 *The wave function, in gray, moving toward the film grains, represented by squares.*

Then, even though the wave function hits all the grains, observation shows that only one of them is activated, as in figure A.2.

FIGURE A.2 *Only one of the grains in figure A.1 is activated even though the electron wave function hits them all. In this example, it is the second (black) one, but different grains will be activated if the experiment is repeated several times.*

Thus the spread-out wave function gives a *localized*—only one grain activated—effect.

Particle explanation. The explanation given for this localizing effect in the particle interpretation is that, hidden within the wave, is an actually existing, very small electron, as in figure A.3. It is this electron that hits and activates a single grain.

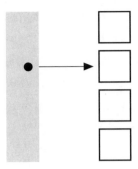

FIGURE A.3 *The particle explanation of figure A.2. The black dot represents a small electron reputedly carried along by the wave function. The reputed electron hits and exposes only one film grain (the second one, to the right of the arrow, in this case).*

COUNTERARGUMENT

The counterargument closely follows the logic of the Stern-Gerlach experiment in which there were two paths for the wave function. In this experiment, there are four possible paths for the wave function, one for each grain. To see this, we divide the wave function into four parts as in figure A.4. Each of these parts follows

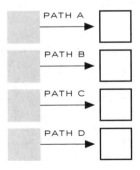

FIGURE A.4 *The wave function of figure A.1 is broken up into four parts, each represented by a gray square. The different parts of the wave function follow different paths, as indicated by the arrows. Each part will hit a different film grain. (Figure A.5 gives a more accurate representation of the mathematics.)*

its own path, as is indicated by the arrows. (The paths of the four parts are close together and parallel here, so they look different from the diverging paths of the Stern-Gerlach experiment. Nevertheless, they still qualify as separate paths.) But the mathematics of quantum mechanics requires that when the wave function breaks into different parts that go their own ways, each part must be represented by a different diagram (as in figure 7.8). Thus figure A.4 is correctly redrawn as in figure A.5.

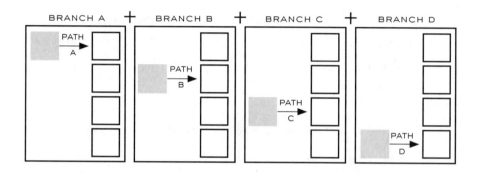

FIGURE A.5 *A drawing, which accurately represents the mathematics, of the four parts of the wave function (gray squares) about to hit their respective film grains. Each part, that is, each path, corresponds to a branch. The four parts are added together to give the wave function.*

Then, once all the different parts of the wave function hit their respective grains, the wave function becomes that of figure A.6 (analogous to figure 7.9).

Therefore, because only one grain is exposed per branch, and because we perceive only one branch (branch B is perceived in figure A.2), we will perceive only one localized grain as being exposed, even though the wave function hit all four grains.

What was used in this derivation of localization? Only the mathematics of quantum mechanics, pictorially represented in figures A.5 and A.6, plus the assumption of only-one perception. (There was no assumption that particles exist.)

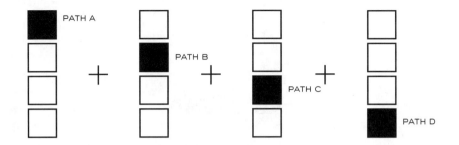

FIGURE A.6 *After the wave function hits the grains, one grain is exposed on each branch, with the exposed grains shown in black. Only one branch is perceived, so only one grain will be perceived as activated, no matter which branch is perceived.*

To help you evaluate this argument, I need to explain what is and what is not controversial in it. Both figures A.5 and A.6 are correct pictorial representations of the mathematics; there is no controversy among physicists here. There is also no controversy about the fact that we see only one branch and that we therefore see only one grain exposed.

The controversy is in *why* we see only one branch. The explanation *could* be that particles exist and we see only the branch that the particle traveled on, but there is no evidence in this or any other quantum-branching experiment that that is the correct explanation of only-one perception. Thus, localization is just one more example of seeing only one branch. It does not tell us why we see only one branch, and it does not show that particles exist, hidden within the wave function.

AN EVALUATION OF QUANTUM MECHANICS

Two of my primary goals are, first, to show that quantum mechanics is compatible with the existence of a nonphysical component to existence, and, second, to show that quantum mechanics can give us valuable information on the nature of the nonphysical aspect. These goals would not be worthwhile if there were a reasonable chance that quantum mechanics might be superseded by an entirely different theory. In my estimation, however, the probability that quantum mechanics will be superseded is very small, for the following reasons:

NO EVIDENCE AGAINST QUANTUM MECHANICS

There is no instance where quantum mechanics gives an answer that is in conflict with any experiment.[1] Thus, there is no experimental evidence that a substantially modified theory is needed.

CLASSICAL PHYSICS

Classical physics, with all its successes—orbits of the planets, engineering applications, and so on—can be derived from quantum mechanics.

MANY SUCCESSES OF QUANTUM MECHANICS

Quantum mechanics has been used to successfully describe and predict an enormous number of extremely diverse phenomena. These include:

- The light spectrum and chemical properties of the elements.
- The properties of the semiconductors used in computers and other electronic equipment. (Thirty percent of the U.S. economy now depends on quantum-related devices!)
- The highly counterintuitive influence-at-a-distance results of the Aspect experiment (see chapter 9).
- The properties of nuclei, from which follow nuclear energy and an accurate description of the life cycles of stars.
- And finally, an accurate description of many of the properties of subatomic particles, including antiparticles, the behavior of quarks, and a systematic classification of the large number of particles that have been discovered.

UNITY

There are only three forces that apply to particles on the atomic and subatomic levels: electromagnetism, weak forces (which apply to nuclear decays), and the strong forces that hold the nucleus together. Electromagnetism and the weak forces appear on the surface to be very different, but they have been beautifully unified into a single electroweak force.[2]

With the advent of the ideas of quarks and gluons,[3] both the nuclear force and the properties of the many elementary particles have been incorporated into a highly unified theory, the theory of the strong interactions. Physics is so unified that there are now essentially only four equations from which all of atomic and particle physics follows. And if one includes the partial successes of grand unified theories,[4] there is some evidence that there are only two equations (one for fermions, such as electrons and quarks, and one for bosons, such as photons and gluons).

LINEARITY

The most basic property of quantum mechanics is that all its equations are linear.[5] This linearity is the essential property for our metaphysical considerations, because it is what allows there to be many potential futures. There is overwhelming support for linearity.

- All the equations that yield the successful predictions of quantum mechanics are linear.
- Interference phenomena occur only for those processes that can be described by linear equations. Therefore the interference phenomena observed for light, electron waves, and so on argue strongly for the linearity of the theory.
- The mathematical discipline of group representation theory, which is applicable only when the equations of a theory are linear, is central to quantum mechanics. Through group representation theory, the most basic properties of matter—mass, energy, momentum, spin, and (through the internal symmetry group) charge—are seen to be a consequence of the linearity of the equations of quantum mechanics, plus relativity. This very tight interlock between linearity, relativity, group representation theory, and the particlelike properties is as close as one can get to a proof that the basics of quantum mechanics will never be superseded or found to be incorrect.

My conclusion is that because of the unity, breadth of successful applications, lack of contradictory evidence, and internal consistency, there is little chance that quantum mechanics will be replaced by another theory. There might be changes to specific equations, there might be another layer or two of elementary particles yet to be discovered, and there might even be a different form for quantum mechanics (see note 3, chapter 9). But I believe there is an end to the theory of the *physical* universe and that we are close to that end.

UNITY IN PHYSICS—ELECTRICITY, MAGNETISM & LIGHT

One of the overriding themes in both mysticism and physics is that of unity and diversity. This is wonderfully illustrated in physics by the theory of electromagnetism. The example also helps us understand the essence of unity and diversity in mysticism.

HISTORY

Historically, the mathematical understanding of electromagnetic theory was based on the separate theories of electricity and magnetism. In the eighteenth century, Charles Coulomb deduced the force law between charged objects. A little later, Jean Baptiste Biot and Felix Savart deduced the magnetic force law. In the early 1800s, a connection was found between electricity and magnetism; an electric current produces a magnetic field, and a changing magnetic field produces an electric current.

Then in 1859, James Clerk Maxwell considered the equations for electricity and magnetism together. He found they could be combined in such a way that they yielded an equation for a wave. The equation was such that the speed of the wave was completely determined by the known constants from the electric and magnetic force laws. When Maxwell calculated this speed, he found it to be 186,000 miles per second, which is exactly the measured speed of light! Light was therefore seen to be an electromagnetic wave, consisting of both an oscillating electric wave and an oscillating magnetic wave. Thus, a great unification had been achieved; electricity, magnetism, and light were all seen to be different aspects of a single theory, now known as electromagnetism.

THE ELECTROMAGNETIC WAVE EQUATION & UNITY

The unity of the electromagnetic theory of light, which consists of only a single equation,[6] is astonishing. This single equation can have many different solutions, each corresponding to a different physical situation. To appreciate how many different phenomena this equation unifies, note that light waves, or more graphically, light rays, can have many different characteristics. For example, one ray of light might be in Los Angeles, another in Boston; one might be weak, another strong; one might be yellow, another blue; one might be traveling north, another west; one might be from the sun, another from a bonfire. Each of these light rays has different physical characteristics—color, strength, direction, origin, location—but they all obey the *same* equation.

The unifying power of this equation extends further still. It is found experimentally that X rays, the microwaves from your oven, and radio waves all travel at the same speed as light. And in fact, they all obey the same wave equation as light! This is indeed unity—so many different phenomena described by a single equation!

UNITY & DIVERSITY

The *unity* in the previous example comes from the *single equation*. The *diversity* comes from the *many solutions* to the equation. The insight into unity and diversity is that the unity—represented here by the equation—is in a different category from the diverse phenomena—represented by the solutions. The same holds true in mysticism; Pure Intelligence is in a different category from all our individual intelligences, so we cannot understand it in the same way. That is, we can think of Pure Intelligence as the *principle* of intelligence, with each Mind being a particular exemplar or application of the principle.

FURTHER THOUGHTS ON THE BRAIN & THE MIND

I will continue here the discussion of free choice, and the link, via the brain, between the physical and nonphysical aspects of existence that I began in chapter 11.

WHAT "FREE" MEANS

In figure 11.6, the Mind has freely chosen to concentrate its awareness on visualizing a tree. What does *free* mean? It has a narrow meaning in this book; it means there are no mathematical or physically mechanistic restrictions on the choice of thought or action. It may be that the Mind has habits or desires that make its choices not so free. But that is not the meaning we give to *free* here when we say *free choice* or *free will*; the meaning refers only to mathematical and physically mechanistic restrictions.

FREE CHOICE & THE LAWS OF PHYSICS

If we were stuck with classical physics (and probably with any theory in which there are objectively existing particles), the mechanism for free choice would involve pushing matter out of its classical deterministic path, thereby contravening the mathematical laws of Nature. That is not acceptable.

But the Mind interpretation of quantum mechanics does not have that problem, for in choosing a branch, no physical law is violated or superseded. The mathematics is not contravened, and all the laws of physics—conservation of energy, and so on—are satisfied for each branch. Thus, the Mind interpretation is ideally suited to free choice with no violation of physics principles.

FREE CHOICE & COMPLEXITY

Our free choice scheme seems complex because the Mind perceives many potential thoughts, but we can argue that *a comparable complexity would occur even if the free choice were implemented by some means other than quantum mechanics.*

To make this clearer, suppose we analyze free choice in a way that is independent of quantum mechanics. There must be choices, and there must be a perceiver of those choices, so there must be a diagram comparable to figure 11.5. Then the perceiver decides which potential thought to concentrate on, so there must be a diagram comparable to figure 11.6. Thus, *there must be diagrams comparable to figures 11.5 and 11.6 whether quantum mechanics is the mechanism for free choice or not,* for the complexity of perceiving several potential thoughts and then choosing between them is inherent in free choice.

QUANTUM MECHANICS & THE BRAIN

In drawing figures 11.3 through 11.6, I have assumed that quantum mechanics is relevant to the brain. I can give a general argument that this is correct, even though the quantum mechanics of the brain, with its trillions and trillions of atoms, is too complicated to analyze exactly.

CLASSICAL DETERMINISTIC MECHANICS & THE BRAIN

First, let's consider the standard argument *against* quantum mechanics being applicable. Many neuroscientists say the brain is a classical, deterministic system, one for which quantum mechanics, with its associated branch structure, is irrelevant. Their reasoning is that the workings of the brain consist essentially of the electrochemical pulses that travel down the neuron, and that these neural pulses are completely described by classical physics. Therefore, say these neuroscientists, quantum mechanics is not relevant.

RELEVANCE OF QUANTUM MECHANICS

I agree with everything in these two statements, but the catch is in the word *essentially*. The electrochemical pulses as they travel down the neuron are indeed governed by deterministic classical physics, but it is at the *boundary* between two neurons, when the pulse jumps from one neuron to another, that quantum mechanics becomes relevant.

This boundary, called the synapse, is very small, less than one hundred atoms wide. And when processes take place over these relatively short distances, we cannot rule out the possibility that a quantum mechanical description, with its many branches, is relevant.[1]

FROM SYNAPSE QUANTUM STATE TO BRAIN QUANTUM STATE

The synapses occupy a special place in the operation of the brain. Because they determine whether a pulse will jump from one neuron to another, they are control points, points that determine the flow of neural pulses. Thus, if there are two quantum branches at each synapse, corresponding to the pulse either jumping or not jumping across, then the wave function of the brain as a whole, with its many billions of synapses, will consist of billions upon billions of quantum branches. And each of these branches will correspond to a particular neural firing pattern and thus to a potential thought or action. This completes the justification for claiming that quantum mechanics is relevant to the brain.

THE ABSTRACTNESS & COMPLEXITY OF PERCEPTION & THOUGHT

There is a potential objection to the Mind interpretation having to do with complexity. The brain is extraordinarily complex, with a hundred billion neurons, each of which is composed of a billion billion atoms. The Mind is presented with the task of making sense of the incredibly complex wave function of all these atoms. Some might say that it is impossible for the Mind to carry out such a complex task and throw out the Mind interpretation on those grounds.

The counterargument is to consider the brain from a materialist's point of view for a moment. There are still a hundred billion neurons. Perception and thought correspond to various patterns of neural pulses, patterns that are both abstract—bearing little direct resemblance to the thought or object of perception they represent—and complex, for they are spread over many hundreds of thousands of neurons.

In spite of this complexity, the brain *does* make sense of these abstract patterns of neural firing. It does this by means of an amazing organizational structure, a structure that evolved over millions of years. Because we are aware only of the end result, we are not consciously aware of the structure or the complex, abstract processing that goes into perceiving our morning toast or thinking about the stock market. But it goes on nevertheless.

THE MACRO STRATEGY

In spite of the fact that each neuron consists of so many atoms, the decoding task facing the Mind is not that much more complex and abstract than that facing the physical brain, provided the Mind uses a "macro" strategy. (In computer programming, several simple instructions can be lumped together into a group, or macro, which can then be thought of as a single instruction on its own. Also see appendix D.) In that strategy, the Mind does not perceive the wave function of each atom individually. Instead it perceives the wave function of each whole neuron all at once, so it pays attention only to "firing" or "not firing," rather than to all the details. If this macro method is used, it is really no more amazing that the Mind can make sense of the wave function of the brain than it is that the physical brain can make sense of the complex, abstract patterns of neural pulses.

FURTHER DJINN THOUGHTS

In this appendix, I have gathered together three additional ideas related to the djinn plane: atoms of djinn thought, the brain and the (djinn) Mind, and the relation between the djinn plane and physical life.

ATOMS OF DJINN THOUGHT

Many of the ideas relevant to the djinn plane are far from our everyday conscious experience, so we must make use of metaphors in explaining them. I will use a chemistry metaphor to clarify the structure of the djinn plane. There is a risk in doing this; the use of metaphoric concepts from the physical plane may prematurely set your "knowing" before you have a real experiential understanding. Even with this risk, including this material still seems worthwhile because it provides a means of unifying the characteristics of the djinn plane.

The chemistry metaphor uses the idea of atoms of djinn thought. As far as I know, this idea is not well developed in the mystical literature. The treatment here is based on a few remarks in the written and oral tradition that suggest that there are basic units of djinn thought.

THE ATOMS OF THE DJINN PLANE

Just as the myriad objects of the physical plane are compounded from elementary particles and atoms, so also we can think of the myriad thought-forms of the djinn plane as being compounded from a few basic djinn thoughts. These basic djinn thought-forms will be called djinn atoms.

I do not know precisely what the atoms of djinn thought are, but to illustrate the idea, I will make a guess. I will assume there are five atoms or elements, analogous to the five alchemical elements. (In the more valid of the ancient traditions, the alchemical elements were not meant to refer to physical elements; the physical elements were only symbols, the nearest analogies one could find to convey what the true alchemical elements are like.) The conjectured significance of each of these elements is given following. These meanings were chosen with the idea in mind that all the forms and intelligent structures of djinn and physical existence could be built from them (and they may therefore not correspond to the usual meanings associated with these elements).

- *Earth.* Form, structure (the precursor of space, nounlike)
- *Water.* Sequence (the precursor of time)
- *Fire.* Emotion, energy, action, intelligence (verblike)
- *Air.* Hierarchy, combination, potential
- *Ether.* Essence, evaluation (adjectivelike)

Ether might also be thought of as that which is passed down from the angelic to the djinn plane. This would include the basic emotions and the attributes—mastery, insight, beauty, and so on.

(The linguist Noam Chomsky has proposed that languages universally have the same structure because that structure is built, or "hardwired," into the structure of the brain. My choice of the five basic djinn elements suggests that we might go one step further and speculate that language has a noun-verb-adjective structure because *existence* has a noun (form)–verb (action, intelligence)–adjective (qualities, emotional evaluation) structure).

DJINN CHEMISTRY

DJINN MOLECULES

Djinn atoms can be combined to create djinn molecules. Not all combinations result in useful molecules. What does *useful* mean here? To answer this, one must remember that djinn molecules are perceived by Minds as djinn thoughts. Some of them will be useful to these Minds while others will not, just as combining hydrogen and oxygen is useful because it yields water, while attempting to combine argon and neon gives no useful compound. The useful combinations are the ones that can be used to build an interesting, fruitful structure of existence, a structure that could aid in achieving the goals of existence.

These useful djinn molecules will quickly become long and complex. As an analog on the physical plane, you might think of the billions of genomes that determine the hereditary characteristics of the human body. These long chains are constructed solely from four protein molecules whose names are abbreviated by A, G, T, and C. These chains differ from each other only in the sequence, the ordering, of the four basic molecules.

DJINN GLUE

What is the glue that holds djinn molecules together? There are no physical forces, of course, because they are not in a physical realm. What holds them together—or better, what makes them a unit, a viable djinn thought—is the individual and collective interest and attention that the djinn Minds of human and other beings give to them. (See the example of calculus in chapter 21.)

DJINN CHEMISTRIES

The chains of thought molecules divide into different chemistries, just as you can have carbon-based chemistries and silicon-based chemistries in the physical world. Each "chemistry" corresponds to a different type of existence (physical existence is only one type of existence), for { } is always searching for any "form" that can be used by Minds to advance toward the goals of existence.

This chemical analogy correctly conveys something of the structure of the djinn plane, but as with all analogies, we must use caution. The molecules, of course, don't actually exist in three-dimensional space; they are more abstract than that. Also, the use of a scientific analogy might make the djinn plane sound dispassionate, but nothing could be further from the truth. There is an immense emotional content on this plane, far more than most human beings can stand. Glimpsing even a small part is staggering.

THE MIND-BRAIN CONNECTION

The ideas in this section are not found in the written or oral traditions of the mystics because there have not been any fully developed mystics who have known the details of modern physics and neuroscience (although Buddha, Padmasambhava, and others no doubt had some grasp—in broad outline but not in detail—of the relation between physical brain intelligence and nonphysical intelligence). Instead, these ideas express how I see quantum mechanics, neuroscience, and the djinn plane fitting together.

There are two aspects to the Mind-brain problem (with Mind here referring to the djinn part of the Mind, which is, for our purposes here, the main aspect of the Mind). The first aspect is to separate brain intelligence from

Mind intelligence. And the second aspect is to form some idea of what occurs on the djinn plane so the Mind can make sense of the workings of the brain.

BRAIN INTELLIGENCE VERSUS MIND INTELLIGENCE

The basic idea is that the brain is a sophisticated computer that the Mind uses to help it make decisions. To illustrate, suppose an architect has a computer program that, when she gives it certain specifications, will apply the proper engineering principles and give her a finished design based on the specifications. The architect tells the computer to produce three different designs, one basically square, one basically octagonal, and one basically elliptical. The architect then uses her aesthetic (and economic) sense to decide which design is better.

The architect corresponds to the Mind and the computer to the brain. The computer-brain does the nuts and bolts logical work—strictly circumscribed by certain rules—and the architect-Mind has the freedom to make the decisions based on how well each version fulfills the desired goals.

This analogy gives the basic idea of the division of intelligence between brain and Mind, but it is an oversimplification. In reality, the architect-Mind has input to the computer-brain at many points, not just the endpoint, in the decisions made in our everyday world.

THE BRAIN & DJINN THOUGHT-FORMS

In chapter 20, I said that it makes sense to think of the wave function as a specialized djinn thought-form that underlies all the phenomena of the physical plane (which we will continue to call the physical plane, instead of the physical djinn realm). There is also a second kind of djinn thought-form relevant to human beings. This second kind, the *djinn brain* subrealm, has to do with how our Minds make sense out of the wave function.

Making sense is by no means a simple task because the wave function of a living object is extremely complicated; the human body has more than a million billion billion (10^{24}) atoms, and the wave function for a system with as few as a thousand atoms is normally far beyond the capacity of any computer to deal with. Because of this complexity, the only way the Mind can make sense of a wave function as complicated as that of the body-brain is if the Mind looks for general features or patterns, rather than dealing with every detail of the wave function. It is the wave function *patterns* appropriate to living physical beings that exist as thought-forms in the djinn plane; they constitute the second set of djinn thought-forms which are particularly relevant to human beings (with the wave function itself being the first set).

HIERARCHICAL STRUCTURE OF THE DJINN BRAIN SUBREALM

There is a hierarchical structure to the djinn brain subrealm (which might be compared to the way in which the physical brain is organized for visual processes). The raw data are the shapes of the wave functions of the atoms of the brain. The first step in the process whereby the Mind makes sense of the wave function, corresponding to identifying the local lines of contrast in the visual process, is that there must be some djinn thought-form pattern that can be used to distinguish the wave function of a firing neuron from that of a non-firing neuron.

A further step the Mind must perform to make sense of the wave function is to relate certain patterns of neural firing to specific bodily functions. For example, the Mind, partly from the storehouse of djinn thought-forms and partly from experience stored in the physical brain, must be able to associate a certain neural firing pattern with moving the hand.

There would also be relations between certain djinn thought-forms and the more complex neural patterns corresponding to thoughts and the manipulation of thoughts.

One might think of these steps as being like *macros* in computer pro-gramming—a grouping together of many lower-order steps into a single higher-order step (see also appendix C.). The basic macro would be the recog-nition of the wave function patterns of a firing (as opposed to a nonfiring) neuron. Higher-order macros, built from combinations of the basic macro, would be the recognition of patterns of firing neurons that signify perception, bodily movement, or a thought. There will be a hierarchy of djinn-plane macros, with the higher ones being often-used combinations of the lower ones, just as we recognize full words rather than seeing their individual letters.

Because the steps are so complicated, and because each one depends on the step before it, this hierarchy of djinn-plane macros almost certainly evolved, instead of every level of the hierarchy springing into existence at once. This evolution is the subject of the next section.

LIFE, DJINN THOUGHT-FORMS & EVOLUTION
WORKING INSTRUCTIONS FOR THE MIND

There are two primary features of life: a physical form whose wave function is sufficiently complex so that there are many choices of possible actions and a Mind associated with each physical form, with the Mind choosing the most suitable action for the organism. To do this choosing, the Mind must have (fig-uratively) a catalog or table that correlates the properties of the wave function, physical actions (such and such a wave function corresponds to moving the hand to pick a peach), and the desires satisfied by each physical action (hunger in the peach case). This correlation table constitutes the working in-structions for the Mind. It tells the Mind how to manage the body, how to pick the physical action that will attain the desired end. (I am not saying that *all* ac-tions taken by an organism are chosen by the Mind, for there is a large amount of mechanistic functioning and decision-making that is automatically built into the structure of the wave function making up the body of a physical being.) The working instructions are a set of djinn thought-forms, and collectively they form the physical life realm of the djinn plane.

There is a different set of instruction thought-forms for each type of organism—flea, dog—with each set being a subrealm or sub-subrealm of the physical life realm.

EVOLUTION ON THE DJINN PLANE

The djinn thought-forms associated with the working instructions will be exceedingly complex. The strategy almost always used to manage complexity is to set up a hierarchical structure. Because each higher level in a hierarchy depends on the nature of the lower levels of the hierarchy, the hierarchies in nature usually evolve, starting with the lowest and most specific and finally evolving to the highest and most general.

Does evolution fit in with the nature of the djinn plane? Yes. The chemistries or structures of the djinn realms and subrealms do not exist forever, from the beginning to the end of time; they change, they evolve. New combinations of thought-atoms are put together (by the Minds of Beings) to form new djinn thought-form molecules. Old combinations disappear from existence (when no Beings hold them in Mind). This evolution in the djinn realms is in accord with the premise that existence is not predetermined or totally mapped out by { }. Existence evolves, with each succeeding step depending on the previous one.

PHYSICAL EVOLUTION & THE DJINN HIERARCHY OF WORKING INSTRUCTIONS

Presumably the hierarchy of djinn working instructions evolved along with the evolution of physical forms here on earth. So the hierarchically lowest set of working instructions, those that developed first, would have been those for the single cell.[1] But even the single cell is a complex organism, so there would no doubt have been many stages in developing the working instructions which the Mind of a cell uses. The Mind of a cell will probably have relatively little (but not zero) freedom of choice; biochemistry will determine nearly all aspects of a cell's behavior. Nevertheless, a cell working instruction subrealm is necessary.

Next would have come the working instructions for multicellular organisms. These would use the single cell working instructions as a base, but would add, as a second level of the hierarchy, instructions having to do with the coordination of the cells. A third level would develop with the specialization of cells to different organs in the organism. And a separate, fourth level would have developed for the nervous system.

THE CAT SUBREALM

Once the general nervous system level of the hierarchy developed, there would then have been a further specialization for each genus and species. So, for example, there would be a house-cat-brain-working-instruction sub-subrealm of the djinn plane, with the distinguishing characteristics of cat behavior encoded in those instructions.

THE HUMAN SUBREALM

When the level of the human being is reached, the operating instructions and goals for the organism are complex indeed. This complexity, which corresponds to another, higher level of the hierarchy, introduces a new potential; insight and a wide range of choices and actions have been added as new facets of existence. These bring with them the potential for new levels of friendship-intimacy and creativity on the physical plane, intensifying them, extending their range. In addition, the human brain can be—although it seldom is—used as a means for its associated Mind to greatly expand its ability to perceive in the djinn plane, as well as in the angelic plane.

INCARNATION IS COMPLEX

Each of us serves a long apprenticeship in the physical realm of the djinn plane *before* we are born here, assimilating all the knowledge we need to exist on the physical plane. In that apprenticeship, our Minds learn about wave functions, cells, how to operate organs, something of the animal subrealms, and finally the human subrealm. Each part of this long journey leaves its mark on the Mind-soul. To have full knowledge of ourselves, we need to remember something of this process. That is only revealed to mature mystics, but it is still worth contemplating.

POTENTIAL

There is another way to describe what has been added to existence by bringing the human form into being. It gives a clear experiential understanding of "potential" to the associated Mind. Beings without this understanding (cells, cats) are not aware that they can progress toward perception and action in ever higher realms of existence.

PHYSICAL EVOLUTION & DJINN EVOLUTION

The current scientific paradigm is that evolution is driven solely by random mutations, with favored organisms surviving because they are more fit to deal with the physical world. I suggest there is also another driving force; existence, { }'s creation, desires to advance toward more friendship-intimacy, more creativity. So in addition to changes that favor physical survival, changes favoring a more fluid and fruitful means of responding to the longing will also flourish. That is, the overall goals of existence, as well as physical survival, play a role in guiding the course of evolution. But I do not know the actual physical mechanism whereby this nonrandom, friendship-intimacy-creativity–enhancing "force" works.

Which comes first, physical or djinn evolution? My guess would be that the drive first comes from the djinn plane (perhaps { } or a Great Being tentatively sets up djinn plane forms), and then that-which-drives—Pure Emotion—waits to see the results as they play out in a Darwinian way. After observing and digesting these results, Pure Emotion in conjunction with Pure Intelligence again pushes the djinn plane (and therefore the physical plane) evolution in a new creativity-friendship-intimacy–enhancing direction.

THE GIFT OF OUR HUMAN BODIES

The human body has evolved and developed over vast expanses of time. It is most cunningly wrought, so we are able to use it as a vehicle to joyously experience existence and to progress with the potential to become Great Beings. We, the most essential part of our selves, cannot help feeling grateful for this incomparable gift.

ENDNOTES

1. We assume there are no particles (to be defended later) and no collapse of
   the wave function (both particles and collapse require amendments to the
   mathematics of quantum mechanics to complete the description of the
   physical world). We also assume there is a *unique* version of each one of
   us that perceives only one of all the many potential realities allowed by
   quantum mechanics. This is in contrast to the "many-worlds" proposal of
   Paul Everett, who suggested that there are many versions of each of us,
   with each version perceiving one of the many potential realities allowed
   by quantum mechanics.

CHAPTER 3. { } & THE GOALS OF EXISTENCE

1. The term *Pure Intelligence* comes from the book *The Soul Whence and Whither* by Hazrat Inayat Khan.

2. A monk named Padmasambhava brought Buddhism to Tibet in the eighth century. He wrote a short treatise called *The Tibetan Book of the Great Liberation* (edited by W. Y. Evans-Wentz) that is an exposition on Pure Intelligence, which he called *The One Mind*. Padmasambhava was probably more experientially familiar with Pure Intelligence than any human being has ever been. I highly recommend this book, even though it is not easy reading.

CHAPTER 5. PHYSICS, NEUROSCIENCE & MYSTICAL PRACTICES

1. It has been conjectured—in opposition to the scheme given here, where true free-choice intelligence (as opposed to deterministic computerlike intelligence) is completely separate from matter—that matter itself has intelligence. That conjecture would seem to depend on a view of matter not inherent in the *mathematics* of quantum mechanics (where particles don't even exist). It is not clear to me how one would develop such a conjecture into an explicitly physics-grounded, coherent, unified scheme of existence that would mesh with the views of the mystics.

CHAPTER 6. CLASSICAL PHYSICS

1. I will argue later that there is a good chance that atoms and particles do not objectively exist. But even if they don't exist, the concept of atoms and particles is so useful—that is, it is such a good shorthand for a collection of properties—that I will continue to use the words *atoms* and *particles*.

CHAPTER 7. QUANTUM MECHANICS

1. An electron is usually in an atom, but not always. In your TV set, electrons that are not attached to atoms are shot through space from a hot filament to the TV screen.

2. Originally performed in 1920 by Otto Stern (1888–1969) and Walter Gerlach (1889–1979), the experiment showed that electrons can have only two "spin" states. The experiment is actually done on atoms rather than on electrons, but that is not important here.

CHAPTER 9. WAVES VERSUS PARTICLES—THE WAVE PICTURE

1. To help you evaluate this argument, I should note that there is no dispute among physicists in the field about this important point—that mass, energy, momentum, and spin will exist as properties of the wave function and have all their usual particlelike characteristics and consequences, even if particles don't exist. It is a fact that was established with mathematical rigor by the Nobel laureate E. P. Wigner in 1939. (There is also no dispute about the corresponding point about charge.) There has not been, however, an appreciation of how strongly this mathematical fact bears on the question of whether particles exist.

2. See John S. Bell, *Physics,* 1, 195–200, 1964; Alain Aspect, Philipe Grangier, and Gerard Roger, *Physical Review Letters,* 91, 49, 1982.

3. If particles do not exist, it might also be possible that space and time do not exist in the sense we usually think of them existing. For a suggestion of how this might come about, see F. A. Blood, Jr., "A Relativistic Quantum Mechanical Harmonic Oscillator without Space-Time Variables," *Journal of Mathematical Physics* 29, 1389, (1988). In this proposed theory, space and time are byproducts of the relativity of quantum mechanics.

4. See Philip Pearle, "Bound State Excitation, Nucleon Decay Experiments, and Models of Wave Function Collapse," *Physical Review Letters,* 73, 913 (1993).

CHAPTER 10. QUANTUM MECHANICS & THE NONPHYSICAL MIND

1. There is another interpretation in which the wave function is all that exists and all branches continue forever; it is the "many-worlds" interpretation of Everett (1957). The difference between Everett's interpretation and ours— and it is a huge difference—is that he does not assume that only one

branch becomes the effective objective reality. Instead he assumes that there is a *different version* of each of us that perceives *each branch*. Because there is no decision made about which branch to perceive, this approach does not explain free will, and so I do not consider it here.

2. One can show *within the bounds of quantum mechanics,* by a method called decoherence theory, that each version of the brain will perceive only one branch rather than a mixture, but decoherence theory cannot explain why only one version is singled out to be conscious, or equivalently, why there is only one "real you."

3. It is possible that quantum mechanics might radically change its form but still retain the qualities—linearity, relativistic invariance, and many-possible-futures aspect—that make it suitable for providing a link between the physical and the nonphysical. See the reference in note 3 of chapter 9 for one possibility along this line.

CHAPTER 11. THE BRAIN & THE MIND

1. See Eccles (1993), *How the Self Controls Its Brain* for essentially the same idea.

CHAPTER 12. PROPERTIES OF THE MIND—PURE INTELLIGENCE

1. Several physicists have proposed the existence of individual Minds or an overarching Mind or Pure Intelligence. See Stapp (1988, 1990, 1991), Goswami (1993), and especially Squires (1990).

CHAPTER 14. INTRODUCTION TO THE BRAIN

1. This quote is a variation of one given by Idries Shah in *The Book of the Book* (Shah 1969). The actual passage reads, "When you realize the difference between the container and the contents, you will have knowledge."

CHAPTER 15. THE SYNAPSE

1. The brain's mechanisms and the influence of the nonphysical Mind are intimately linked in our everyday thinking, perception, and experience of emotion. When I say "thought" or "perception" or "emotion" in the brain section, with no qualifier such as nonphysical, I am referring only to the physical, brain-based part of these processes.

2. Antonio Damasio, *Descartes' Error.*

CHAPTER 16. THE COMPUTERLIKE ASPECTS OF THE BRAIN

1. See Joseph LeDoux, *The Emotional Brain.*

2. See the *New York Times.* "Seeing and Imagining: Clues to the Workings of the Mind's Eye," August 31, 1995.

CHAPTER 17. EMOTIONS—CONTROL OF ATTENTION

1. See Gazzaniga, *The Social Brain,* Basic Books, New York, 1985.

CHAPTER 18. THE ANGELIC PLANE—EMOTION

1. Tosun Bayrak, *The Most Beautiful Names.*

CHAPTER 20. DUALITY, LIFE, COVENANTS

1. An alternative view is that there is a Mind that inhabits each physical object, but the Minds associated with "inanimate" objects have very little say in what happens in our physical world. I prefer the point of view of the main text.

CHAPTER 21. THE DJINN PLANE & MYSTICISM

1. This phenomenon is described in *Consciousness Explained* by Daniel Dennett.

2. Rupert Sheldrake, *A New Science of Life,* Jeremy P. Tarcher, Inc., Los Angeles.

3. There was an isolated island on which monkeys began to wash their food. After a certain number of monkeys (one hundred?) in the original group took up food washing, it spread to groups of monkeys on the other islands that had no contact with the original food washing monkeys.

CHAPTER 22. PRELIMINARIES TO THE PRACTICES

1. It might be helpful to comment on what I mean by the word *perceive*. It is nearly synonymous with *being aware of*. On the physical level, it refers to visual sight, hearing, and so on. On another level, there is what might be called "supernatural" (supraphysical) perception; telepathy, seeing the future, seeing auras, and so on. But perception is meant to go beyond even that. The aim of the mystic is to be aware of the full sweep of existence.

2. This categorization is given in *Divinity of the Human Soul* by H. I. Khan, (1990).

CHAPTER 23. THE WATCHING-YOUR-THOUGHTS PRACTICE

1. See *The Miracle of Mindfulness* by Thich Nhat Hanh for an excellent description of this practice.

CHAPTER 24. BREATH, MUSIC & THE CHAKRAS

1. Pir Vilayat Inayat Khan, *That Which Transpires Behind That Which Appears*.
2. Reps, Paul, *Zen Flesh, Zen Bones*.
3. Quotes from H. I. Kahn, *Music*. The Sufi Publishing Co.
4. Hafiz.

CHAPTER 25. PRACTICES PERFORMED DURING EVERYDAY LIFE

1. *Science News*, Sept. 25, 1999, Vol. 156, 205–207. Also, for an excellent book on sleep, see Dement, 1999.

2. These mindset practices were devised by the contemporary Sufi teacher, Shahabuddin David Less.

3. "Toward the One" and "United with All" come from the Invocation of Hazrat Inayat Khan.

4. The Dalai Lama.

5. *That Which Transpires Behind That Which Appears* is the title of a book by Pir Vilayat Inayat Khan.

CHAPTER 26. THE ART OF THE SELF

1. Quoted from the Dhammapada in *The Divinity of the Human Soul* by Hazrat Inayat Khan.

2. See Inayat Khan's book *The Art of Personality*.

3. Hazrat Inayat Khan, *Mastery Through Accomplishment*.

4. Idries Shah, *The Exploits of the Incredible Mulla Nasrudin*.

5. Idries Shah, *Caravan of Dreams, Wisdom of the Idiots,* and *World Tales.*

6. *The Tibetan Book of the Great Liberation,* by W. Y. Evans-Wentz.

CHAPTER 29. THE MYSTIC & SOCIETY

1. This idea is from a talk by Shahabuddin David Less.

2. For documentation of potential trouble spots, see *Vital Signs 2001* (Brown 2001), a compilation by the Worldwatch Institute of world trends.

3. Idries Shah, *World Tales*.

4. This description is primarily from a lecture by Shahabuddin David Less.

5. From a talk by Pir Vilayat Inayat Khan.

APPENDIX B. AN EVALUATION OF QUANTUM MECHANICS

1. There are three areas that are currently problematic for quantum mechanics. First, infinities occur in the calculation of certain quantities. However, using care, these infinities can be made to cancel out in a systematic way, and the correct answers follow. It is thought that these infinity problems occur because the strategy used for the calculations is awkward, rather than because the basic premises of quantum mechanics are incorrect.

Second, the observation of the number of neutrinos per second from the sun is much smaller than predicted. The current thinking is that this results from an inadequate understanding of the theory of neutrinos, rather than from a basic failure of quantum mechanics. New experimental results show that when all three types of neutrinos are accurately detected, quantum mechanics gives the correct results after all. (See, for example, *Scientific American*, Sept. 2001, page 18.) Thus quantum mechanics is vindicated once again.

Third, no way has yet been found to integrate the gravitational force into quantum mechanics, but there is no indication that this implies that either the linearity or the relativistic invariance of quantum mechanics is incorrect.

2. See Howard Georgi and Sheldon Glashow, *Physics Today*, September 1980, for an explanation of the unified electroweak theory.

3. Protons and neutrons are each made up of three quarks, so quarks are sub-nuclear particles. The gluons "carry" the strong force between quarks, just as photons "carry" the electromagnetic force between charged particles.

4. See Steven Weinberg, *The Quantum Theory of Fields*.

5. The equation

$$3x+5=17$$

is a linear equation for the unknown x; but the equation

$$3x^2+5=17$$

is a nonlinear equation for x, because x is multiplied by itself.

6. Actually, there are four equations in electromagnetic theory, not just one, but that is not relevant to our argument here.

APPENDIX C. FURTHER THOUGHTS ON THE BRAIN & THE MIND

1. In particular, Stapp (1993) has given a strong argument, involving the quantum spread of calcium ions, to show that the branch structure of quantum mechanics is indeed relevant at the synapse.

APPENDIX D. FURTHER DJINN THOUGHTS

1. See Goodenough (1998) for a clear explanation of evolution in relation to the cell.

BIBLIOGRAPHY

Bayrak, Sheikh Tosun (1985). *The Most Beautiful Names.* Threshold, Putney.

Brother Lawrence (1977). *The Practice of the Presence of God.* translated by John J. Delaney, Doubleday, New York.

Brown, Lester (2001). *Vital Signs, 2001.* W. W. Norton. New York.

Damasio, Antonio R. (1994). *Descartes' Error.* Putnam, New York.

Dement, William C. (1999). *The Promise of Sleep.* Dell, New York.

Dennett, Daniel C. (1991). *Consciousness Explained.* Little Brown, Boston.

Eccles, John C. (1994). *How the SELF Controls its BRAIN.* Springer-Verlag, Berlin.

Goodenough, Ursula (1998). *The Sacred Depths of Nature.* Oxford University Press, Oxford.

Goswami, Amit (1993). *The Self-Aware Universe.* Tarcher/Putnam, New York.

Hafiz (1996). *I Heard God Laughing,* translated by Daniel Ladinsky. Dharma Printing Company, Oakland.

Hanh, Thich Nhat (1987). *The Miracle of Mindfulness.* Beacon Press, Boston.

Hooper, Judith, and Teresi, Dick (1986). *The 3-Pound Universe.* Macmillan, New York.

Ibn Arabi (1985?). *Kernel of the Kernel,* translated by Ismail Hakki Bursevi. Beshara Publications, Gloucestershire, England.

Khan, Hazrat Inayat (1982). *The Art of Personality.* Omega Publications, New Lebanon.

Khan, Hazrat Inayat (1978). *Mastery Through Accomplishment.* Omega Press, New Lebanon.

Khan, Hazrat Inayat (1984). *The Soul Whence and Whither.* East-West Publications, Middlesex, England.

Khan, Hazrat Inayat (1990). *The Divinity of the Human Spirit.* Shri Jainendra Press, Delhi, India.

Khan, Inayat (1995). *Creating the Person.* Omega Publications, New Lebanon.

Khan, Pir Vilayat Inayat (1994). *That Which Transpires Behind That Which Appears.* Omega Press, New Lebanon.

Khan, Pir Vilayat Inayat (1999). *Awakening.* Tarcher Putnam, New York.

Khan, Sufi Inayat (1977). *Music.* Samuel Weiser, New York.

Lao-Tzu (1991). *Tao Te Ching.* translated by Stephen Mitchell, HarperCollins, New York.

LeDoux, Joseph (1996). *The Emotional Brain.* Simon and Schuster, New York.

Padmasambhava (1954). *The Tibetan Book of the Great Liberation,* edited and translated by W. Y. Evans-Wentz. Oxford, London.

Reps, Paul, Nyogen Senzaki (1994). *Zen Flesh, Zen Bones.* Shambhala Publications Inc., Boston.

Rinpoche, Sogyal (1992). *The Tibetan Book of Living and Dying.* HarperSanFrancisco, San Francisco.

Rumi, Jelaluddin, (1994). *The Essential Rumi,* translated by Coleman Barks. HarperSanFrancisco, San Francisco.

Shah, Idries (1969). *Wisdom of the Idiots.* E. P. Dutton, New York.

Shah, Idries (1969). *The Book of the Book.* Octagon Press, London.

Shah, Idries (1972). *The Exploits of the Incomparable Mulla Nasrudin.* E. P. Dutton, New York.

Shah, Idries (1979). *World Tales.* Harcourt Brace Jovanovich, New York.

Shah, Idries (1995). *Caravan of Dreams.* Octagon Press, London.

Sheldrake, Rupert, (1995). *A New Science of Life.* Inner Traditions, Rochester, VT.

Squires, Euan J., *Quantum Theory and the Relation between Conscious Mind and the Physical World.* University of Durham perprint DTP–90/50.

Stapp, Henry P. (1993). *Mind, Matter, and Quantum Mechanics.* Springer-Verlag, Berlin.

Suzuki, Shunryu (1970). *Zen Mind, Beginner's Mind.* Weatherhill, New York.

Weinberg, Steven (1995). *The Quantum Theory of Fields.* Cambridge University Press, Cambridge.

INDEX

{ }
  definition, 30
  Hu, 30
  humans not puppets of, 32
  imperfection, 34
  mathematics, 44
  perspective on physical existence, 44
  relation of human beings to, 33

A

abstract
  pattern of pulses, 117
  perception and thought, 286
active disinterest, 175
adenosine, 125
alchemical elements
  breaths, 214
  djinn atoms, 289
amygdala, 138
angelic plane, 154–156
  forms, 154
  intelligence, 155
  power, 155
anger
  after death, 160
  mindset practice, 223
  neurochemistry, 125
  source of energy, 224

areas of the brain
  vision, 126–130
art of the self, 229–246, 259
association
  neurochemicals, 145
  restricts freedom of thought, 145
atoms of djinn thought, 289
attention
  brain processes, 140–144
attributes of existence, 156
  (see also qualities)
  beauty, 242–244
  insight, 238–242
  friendship, 264
  mastery, 233–238
awareness
  materialist's and mystic's views, 143
  nonconscious control, 144
  practices, 219
  pure awareness, 221
axon, 120
axonic pulse, 121

B

bardo of becoming, 36
beauty, 242–244
Bell Aspect result, 79
bhakti, 190, 226, 242

billiard ball universe, 53
blindsight, 172
book
    advantage, 153, 186
Brahe, Tycho, 239
brain
    abstract decoding, 127
    computerlike, 127
    feelings, 139
    helps us grow, 253
    holds us back, 254
    instrument, 253
    Mind, 95–98, 283–287, 291
    mysticism, 115–116
    quantum mechanics, 96–98, 285
brain functions
    practices, 199
brain intelligence vs Mind intelligence, 292
brain wave function
    choice, 99–100
    determinism, 99
    organization, 119
branches
    choosing mechanism, 69
    many possible futures, 68
    perception of only one, 66
    Stern-Gerhach experiment, 66
    thoughts, 96
breath
    cautions, 204
    chakras, 213
    everyday life, 206
    fire, 214, 238
    health, 208
    metaphor for { }, 203
    others, 207
    state, 207
    theory, 203
    thoughts, 206
    watching the breath, 205
Brother Lawrence, 225–226

C
caffeine, 124
calculus, 174
cerebral cortex
    areas, 126

chains of thought
    association, 256
    determinism, 100
    emotions, 145
    microemotions, 147
chakras, 211
    breath, 213
    functions, 212
    location, 211
    sounds, 212
chanting, 210, 258
chemistry metaphor, 288
choice—see free choice
    in the brain wave function, 99–100
choosing mechanism
    not known in quantum mechanics, 69
clairvoyance, 176
Claperede, 132
clarity, 241
classical physics, 53
    derivable from quantum mechanics, 57
    inadequate, 57
collapse interpretation, 80
complexity
    incarnation, 294
    perception and thought, 286
computer, 43
    aspect of brain, 128
    macro, 287, 294
    not alive, 166
concepts
    { } is beyond, 204
    djinn thought-forms, 37
    limitation, 256
    Mindsets, 149
    patterns of neural pulses, 117
    relation to memory, 135
cosmology, 19–21
covenants, 167
creative imagination
    intuition, 177
creativity,
    breath, 207
    goals of existence, 31
    imagination, 177
    intuition, 134, 197
    payoff, 201

play, 236
response to longing, 243
restrictions, 163
watching-your-thoughts
  practice, 197, 198
workplace, 264

D
Damasio, 125, 138
death
  emotions after death, 160
  existence after death, 181
decision-making
  emotions, 138
dendrite, 120
Descartes
  dualism, 81
determinism
  body, 73
  brain wave function, 99
  freedom of choice, 74
  mathematical, 53
  no free will, 55
  physical, 54
development of the self practice, 189
diversity
  {, 30
  nature, 31
  physics, 209
  unity, 282
djinn atoms, 288–291
djinn mind, 170
djinn plane, 35–39
  chemistry metaphor, 288
  clairvoyance, 176
  genius, 173
  glue, 290
  life before birth, 38
  life on earth, 37
  mind reading, 173
  realms, 37, 169–170
  *The Tibetan Book of Living and
    Dying,* 36
  types of beings, 170
djinn plane knowledge
  intuition, 173
  ordinary life, 171

djinn thought-forms, 36, 169
  atoms, 288
dreams
  level of attention, 143
  practice, 219
  visual imaging, 135
duality, dualism
  Descartes, 81
  unity, 26
  wave-particle, 80
  wave function part of djinn plane, 166

E
ego, 231
emotions
  amygdala, 138
  brain, 137
  decision making, 138
  feelings, 139, 158
  giving up, 159
  guide our thinking, 137
  hierarchical structure, 158
  motivation, 158
  neurochemistry, 125
  secondary, 159
enlightenment, 177
equations of quantum mechanics
  definition of physical universe, 209
  not overruled, 81
  only two, 42, 280
  particles not mentioned, 79
  Schrödinger, 59
  unity-diversity, 209
Evans-Wentz, 242
everyday life practices, 220–228
evolution,
  djinn plane, 294–295
  physical, 295
existence
  division into physical and non-
    physical, 24

F
feelings, 139
forms of existence, 36
  angelic, 154
  djinn, 36

free will
    Mind interpretation, 91
free choice, 99–100
    body, 74
    complexity, 284
    laws of physics, 284
    meaning of free, 283
    synapses, 74
friendship, 264
    derivative, distorted forms, 159
    goal of existence, 31
    the mystic, 264
    quality of existence, 31

G
Gabriel, 155
genius, 173
gluons, 279
glutamate, 124
goals
    of existence, 31
    of mystic, 261
    of practices, 46, 186, 257
good and bad, 245
Great Beings, 179
group theory, 78, 280

H
Hafiz, 208, 248
healers and healing
    djinn plane, 178
hidden treasure, 31
hierarchy
    djinn atom, 28
    djinn plane, 294
    emotion, 158
    mystical religion, 268
    three planes, 157
Hu
    definition, 30
hundredth monkey phenomenon, 174

I
Ibn Arabi, 230, 269
imagination, 135
imperfection
    { }, 34

incarnation, 161, 297
indifference, 148
individuality, 230
insight, 238–242
    development, 240
    essence, 239
    time, 241
internal symmetry group, 78, 280
interpretations of quantum mechanics, 76
    collapse, 80
    Mind, 90
    particle, 76
intuition
    blindsight, 172
    creative imagination, 177
    distorted by rationalization, 147
    djinn plane, 172
    everyday practice, 226
    feel of, 176
    knowing yourself, 230
    memory categories, 134
    microemotions, 148
    mystical mastery, 230
    nonphysical, 92
    payoff, 201

J
James, William, 139
jihad, 224
journey
    of the soul, 161–168

K
Kepler, Johannes, 239
Khan, Hazrat Inayat, 208, 214, 244
Khan, Pir Vilayat, 204, 230

L
language
    music, 209
LeDoux, 131, 140
Lewis, Samuel, 203, 213
life
    definition, 166
lifetime of thoughts, 175
light beam experiment, 59
linearity, 78, 280

localization
    electron-film example, 273
    explanation, 273–277
    particle interpretation, 78
loneliness, 161, 264
love, 264

M
macro strategy, 174, 287, 294
macroscopic and microscopic
    choice at microscopic level, 72
    definition, 72
many possible futures, 58, 68
mastery, 223–238
    mystical, 237
materialism
    definition, 44
    and mysticism, 75
    no support for in science, 44, 52, 55
    particles, 75
    zeitgeist of our age, 180
mathematics
    { }, 44
    order and freedom, 44
    physics, 52
    quantum mechanics, 42
memory, 131–133
    circuit, 131
    types, 131–133
memory categories, 133
    intuition, 134
    limitation, 133
metaphysics
    physics, 92
microemotions
    description, 139
    intuition, 148
    restricts freedom of thought, 147–148
Mind interpretation, 90
    brain, 95–98
    bridge between physical and non-
        physical worlds, 91
    free will, 91
Mind, nonphysical
    ability to choose thoughts, 26
    archetypal awareness, 106
    brain, 283–287, 291

characteristics, 103
choice, 91, 105
    implied by quantum mechanics,
        85–89
    perceives only the wave function of the
        brain, 89
    self, 104
    working instructions, 294
mind reading
    djinn plane, 173
mind-sets
    acquisition in djinn plane, 37
    after death, 37, 149, 160, 255
    description, 148
    know yourself, 230
    microemotions, 139
    mystical religions, 268
    narrow focus, 46
    purification, 213
    retreats, 258
    zeitgeist, 180
mind-set practices, 231, 255
    anger, 223
    not defending yourself, 224
    no harm to others, 224
    self-pity, 224
    speak no ill, 224
morphogenic fields—see Sheldrake
Muhammad
    Gabriel, 155
    hidden treasure, 31
    practices at night, 218
music, 208–210
    language, 209
    law of universe, 209
    practices, 210
    spirituality, 210
mystic
    description, 190, 249
    goals, 261
mystical practices
    general methods, 46
    goals, 46, 186, 257
mystical religion, 268–269
mystical society of the future, 262
mystical teachers, 249
    djinn plane, 178

mysticism
    brain, 115–116
    conceptual knowledge of, 153
    definition, 25
    duality, 26
    materialism, 75
    science not preclude, 25
    Sufi, 27

N
Nasrudin
    key, 238
    rifle, 236
    wandering at 4:00 A.M., 24
net image, 188
neurochemistry
    emotions, 125
    association, 145
neuron
    axonic pulse, 121
    binary code, 130
    connections, 121
    function, 120–121
neuroscience
    does not imply no soul, 44
neurotransmitters, 123–124
    excitatory and inhibitory, 124
Newton, Isaac, 53
night practices, 218
nonphysical Mind. See Mind.

O
objective reality
    none in quantum mechanics, 68
only-one perception, 69
operating instructions on djinn plane, 167

P
particlelike properties
    quantum mechanics, 77
    wave function, 77
particles
    in classical physics, 54
    localization, 78
    no evidence for, 44
    no particle assumption, 80
    perception of only one branch, 76

perception of only one branch
    particle interpretation, 76
    Stern-Gerlach experiment, 66
physical and nonphysical
    examples, 92
physical existence
    general structure, 45
physical plane
    advantages and disadvantages,
        253–255
    concrete, 254
    mastery, 254
physical universe
    definition, 42, 82
physics
    classical, 53
    experiments, 52
    mathematics, 52
    metaphysics, 92
    reductive aspect, 51
    unity, 51
Plato, 36
potential, 20, 295
practice of the presence of God, 225
    breathing, 227
    intuition, 228
    Kyrie Eleison, 227
    Om Mane Padme Hum, 227
    sacred name, 227
    Toward the One, 227
practices
    art of the self, 229–246
    beauty, 242–244
    brain functions, 199, 257
    breath-chakra practices, 212
    development of the self, 189
    everyday life practices, 220–238
    goals, 46, 186, 257
    insight, 238–242
    knowing yourself, 230
    mastery, 233–238
    mindset, 223
    music, 210
    neutral and positive strategies, 188
    presence of God, 225
    purification breaths, 213
    range of awareness, 173

rhythm, 196, 199
schedule, 195, 231
traditional paths/yogas, 190
walking, 220–222
watching-your-thoughts, 193–201
prefrontal cortex, 143
probability law
Stern-Gerlach experiment, 69
no explanation in Mind
interpretation, 90
programming the universe, 270
psychics, 177
puppet, 32
body as puppet, 45
Mind as puppeteer, 45
Pure Emotion
definition, 30
glue of existence, 158
Pure Intelligence
connections between Minds, 105
creative part of { }, 161
definition, 31, 105
principle of intelligence, 282
relation to individual Mind, 32,
104, 163
purification, 213
purification breaths, 213
Pythagoras, 270

Q
qualities of existence
99 names, 156
angelic plane, 156, 162
quantum logic
light beam experiment, 60
quantum mechanics
amendments, 42
brain, 96–98, 285
evaluation, 278–281
flaw, 25
implies nonphysical Mind, 85–89
interpretations, 76
many possible futures, 58
Mind interpretation, 90
nonphysical aspect to existence, 25
particle interpretation, 76

particlelike properties, 77
quarks, 45, 51, 279
Quran, 156

R
randomness, quantum (see also
probability law)
in light beam experiment, 60
rationalization, 145–146
distorts intuitive information, 147
realms of the djinn plane,
169–170
brain subrealm, 292
form of existence, 169
reincarnation, 38, 163
Reps, Paul, 207
reticular formation, 142
retreats, 247–249, 258
guides, 248
types, 248
Rumi
almost invisible, 270
body nurtures spirit, 253
caravan, 236
circumcision, 37
closer to you than, 104, 163
eye goes blind, 242
fiery insight, 250
how can I be conscious, 100
maid and wife, 231
melting snow, 214
mouse and frog, 265
Muhammed and Gabriel, 155
patient, 217
sleep, 218
soul's journeying, 187
wandering talk, 200
with you always, 225

S
Schrödinger's cat
description of gedankenexperiment, 172
self
Mind, 104
self-confidence, 236
Shah, Idries

teaching tales, 241
  Man with the Wen, 265–266
Sheldrake's morphogenic fields
  djinn plane, 174
  lifetime of thoughts, 174
sleep
  attention mechanism, 142
  creativity, 240
  dreams, 240
  intuition, 176
  practices, 218
Sogyal Rinpoche, 36
sources of deep knowledge, 92
speech, 130
split-brain experiment, 146
Stern-Gerlach experiment
  described, 66
  probability law, 69
subrealms of djinn plane, 170
  brain, 292
  human, 294
Sufism, definition, 27
synapse, 122–124
  efficiency, 124
  quantum mechanics, 73, 96,
    126, 285
  pivotal role, 122
  size, 123, 126
synaptic cleft, 123

T
Tao Te Ching, 30, 230, 250
teacher, 249–251
teaching tales, 241
tennis, 168
thalamus
  attention, 142
thinking
  reduce the amount, 228
thoughts
  branches, 96–98
three-plane nature of human beings, 163
tree-leaf image, 163
Tibetan Book of Living and Dying, 36
time
  insight, 241

U
unity
  diversity, 282
  duality, 26
  electromagnetism, 281
  physics, 51, 279

V
virtue, 243
vision, 128–130
Von Neumann, John, 80

W
watching the breath, 205, 258
watching-your-thoughts practice,
  193–201, 257
  alertness, 199
  creativity, 198
  payoff, 201
  pulling effect on thoughts, 198
  rhythm, 195
  schedule, 195
wave function
  branches, 66
  mist picture, 59
  particlelike properties, 77
  specialized kind of djinn thought-
    form, 166
wave-particle duality, 80
wave picture, 81
wisdom, 242

Z
zeitgeist, 190
Zen Mind, Beginner's Mind, 195

ABOUT THE AUTHOR

Dr. Casey Blood is a Ph.D. in physics from Case Western Reserve. He taught physics for thirty years at Rutgers University. Most of his publications relate to quantum physics. he also taught environmental science at Rutgers, finding himself in increasing disagreement with the modern idea that man is essentially an economic animal. In addition he has done independent research in neuroscience.

Forever twenty years he has been a serious student-practioner of Sufism, the ecstatic mystical tradition that originates in the Middle East. He has also participated in Buddhist and Native American practices for many years and has encountered and been taught by mystics from many traditions around the world.

Dr. Blood writes: "I have looked for a way to unify science and religion for thirty years. To find it, I had to understand quantum physics on the deepest level. . . . And I had to be taught, for a long time, by a teacher from an ancient spiritual tradition who could take me through all the stages I needed to acquire the mystical knowledge necessary to see the unification."